Searching for the Anthropocene

ALSO BY CHRISTOPHER SCHABERG

The Textual Life of Airports: Reading the Culture of Flight (2011)
The End of Airports (2015)
Airportness: The Nature of Flight (2017)
The Work of Literature in an Age of Post-Truth (2018)

Searching for the Anthropocene

A Journey into the Environmental Humanities

Christopher Schaberg

BLOOMSBURY ACADEMIC
NEW YORK • LONDON • OXFORD • NEW DELHI • SYDNEY

BLOOMSBURY ACADEMIC
Bloomsbury Publishing Inc
1385 Broadway, New York, NY 10018, USA
50 Bedford Square, London, WC1B 3DP, UK

BLOOMSBURY, BLOOMSBURY ACADEMIC and the Diana logo are trademarks
of Bloomsbury Publishing Plc

First published in the United States of America 2020

Copyright © Christopher Schaberg, 2020

For legal purposes the Acknowledgments on p. 185 constitute an extension
of this copyright page.

Whilst every effort has been made to locate copyright holders the publishers
would be grateful to hear from any person(s) not here acknowledged.

Cover design: Eleanor Rose
Cover image © Christopher Schaberg

All rights reserved. No part of this publication may be reproduced or
transmitted in any form or by any means, electronic or mechanical,
including photocopying, recording, or any information storage or retrieval
system, without prior permission in writing from the publishers.

Bloomsbury Publishing Inc does not have any control over, or responsibility for,
any third-party websites referred to or in this book. All internet addresses given
in this book were correct at the time of going to press. The author and publisher
regret any inconvenience caused if addresses have changed or sites have ceased
to exist, but can accept no responsibility for any such changes.

A catalog record for this book is available from the Library of Congress.

ISBN: HB: 978-1-5013-5183-9
PB: 978-1-5013-5182-2
ePDF: 978-1-5013-5184-6
eBook: 978-1-5013-5185-3

Typeset by Newgen KnowledgeWorks Pvt. Ltd., Chennai, India

To find out more about our authors and books visit www.bloomsbury.com
and sign up for our newsletters.

For Vera

Contents

List of Figures xi

Part I Home Sick 1

Part II Jet Lag 89

Acknowledgments 183
Reprint Acknowledgments 185
Bibliography 187
Index 195

Time to get up and stare
at wasted space, slow-roasted greenery.
—MAGGIE NELSON

To land is necessarily to land someplace.
—BRUNO LATOUR

Figures

1. The Sleeping Bear Dunes shoreline invites and resists 3
2. Drawing lesson: Anthropocene amalgam 21
3. Even the most generic terminal is key to the Anthropocene 90
4. A simple diagram of a jet engine belies the Anthropocene 115
5. © Texture 2017 169
6. © Star Alliance 2018 178

Part I
Home Sick

Flying over Lake Michigan, if you are heading eastward and you have a window seat, you may be lucky enough to see them: Lurching against crashing surf, several humpback formations made of sand. Millennia in the making.

Sleeping Bear, Still Moving

The Legend of the Sleeping Bear is that there was once a family of three bears who lived in northern Wisconsin. One year there was a terrible wildfire that swept across the state. The bears were driven to the eastern border of the state, where Lake Michigan stretches out to the horizon. The inferno was pressing down on the bears. The mother bear took to the lake, swimming across the wide expanse. Her cubs dove into the surf and swam, too, following their mother's path through the increasingly treacherous swells. Alas, when the mother bear reached the far shore, in Michigan, the cubs were still far behind. The mother bear, exhausted, laid down to rest and wait for her cubs. And she is lying there still, waiting for them: she is the vast Sleeping Bear dune. The cubs are the North and South Manitou Islands, which sit more than 10 miles offshore, their own sandy cliffs visible from the beach. The story is left in strange suspense, as if the islands might one day join the shore. And, of course, given glacial timescales, perhaps they one day *will*.

Growing up I heard this story countless times, always with slight variations. Another version has it that the bear family was migrating to look for food, and that the cubs drowned—and as the mother bear mourned their deaths, the islands rose from the lake almost as gravestones.

This story tugs at the heartstrings of the listener, full as it is of the sadness of exodus and loss, disaster and migration. The legend of the sleeping bear also has curious philosophical implications. One might be tempted to dismiss the story for its brash anthropomorphism, with both the land and the bears imbued with all too human emotions and affects. As if everything is measurable by a human yardstick. And yet, as Jane Bennett points out in her book *Vibrant Matter*, "A touch of anthropomorphism ... can catalyze a sensibility that finds a world filled not with ontologically distinct categories of beings (subjects and objects) but with variously composed materialities that form confederations" (99). Following Bennett, lingering with the myth of the Sleeping Bear we might find *more* here: more than just the human—and importantly less, too.

The myth of the Sleeping Bear blurs the radically different elements involved therein. The dune ecosystem is imagined and animated as an *ursus*, yet through the story the black bears themselves are transmogrified *back* into the landforms that they appear to *be* in the present moment of the story as it is being told. The listener too becomes absorbed in the story, observing the observant sleeping bear, acting as another animal in mortal transit, perhaps as ethereal as the ever-changing clouds above, just on a different timescale. It is a slippery tale, then, where scales shift as dramatically and rapidly as its characters change form. Far from being a quaint legend, this story initiates a comportment of wonder that might be harnessed for generously imagining the myriad existences in this region—and beyond.

What's interesting about this legend is that the sleeping bear is always *still moving*. The prevailing winds blow this massive "perched" dunescape slowly toward the northeast, changing the makeup of the topography gradually but noticeably over time. I remember the steep slope of one particular sand bowl when I was a child, running down it. Now in the same place I see an entirely different curvature, fading off in an obscure way, dune grass encroaching. But is it even right to call this "the same place," moving as it is? Whatever "place" is trembles in this fable, comes to vibrant life.

Likewise, from my family's home across Good Harbor Bay I used to be able to look out at Pyramid Point and see a wide swath of sand; now, some twenty-five years later, that area is patchy with junipers and aspen trees forming redoubts where enough soil has mixed with the moving sand. This view awes and inspires, humbles and intimidates. It is a glimpse of the constantly changing planet, and it renders human pursuits minuscule. Yet, in a reflexive turn, like the retransformations of the Sleeping Bear, it can also animate: it is a stunning arc of shoreline that beckons and yields, calls for, and resists interpretation.

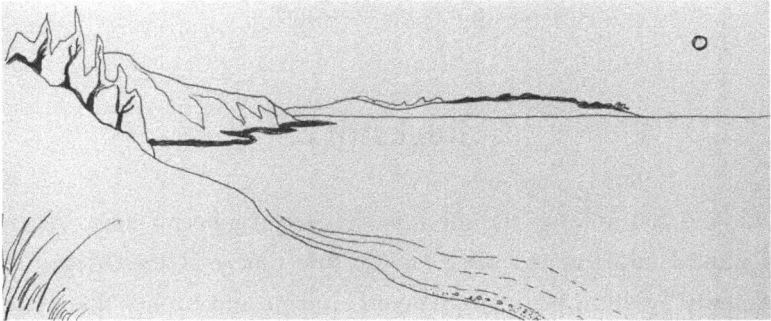

Figure 1 *The Sleeping Bear Dunes shoreline invites and resists. Illustration by Lara Schaberg.*

Closer up, being right in them, the dunes take on liveliness in other ways. There are ghost poplar forests in eerie sand canyons, tendril-like marram grassroots grasping out where a cliff has fallen away, and weird, almost vertical bluffs where the sand plummets down into skeins of wild grapevines or bittersweet snarls, ancient cedar and poplar stumps suddenly exposed. And nearly everywhere on the dunes, if you pause, you can feel the sand gently pelting you. It gets into your hair and covers your scalp if you sit for a mere few minutes. Many months later, back in New Orleans, I'll discover small heaps hidden in my backpack or shoes. The dunes are still moving, in many senses of the word.

And just when the view over the lake looks pure, the dunes framing the blue-green lake in perfection, a long dark freighter will slide into view—exhaust belching from its pulsing engine, whose strange reverberations can be felt in the body from miles away. And if I look down, I'll see other things: plastic shards and tangled synthetic strands. Not so pure, after all. To wander the Sleeping Bear is to invite strange crossings and visions, to become disoriented in what is at once a pristine and tattered edge of the Anthropocene. If this last word is unfamiliar to my reader, please be patient. I won't define Anthropocene immediately, but gradually and provisionally. It's a *search*, one that starts here on the dunes.

Backstory

About 1,200 miles to the south of the Sleeping Bear Dunes: When I walked into the jet bridge for the first time in New Orleans in January 2009, on the seam between airplane and tunnel, this place immediately felt like home. The thick New Orleans air, even in midwinter, poured into the jet bridge and enveloped me.

One of the things I have noticed about living here for ten years now is the unsettling blend of decrepitude and rejuvenation, grittiness and new construction. These dualities always have their upsides and downsides, depending on where you are on any given night or day—not to mention where you have to sleep. Yet the overall sensation, at least for me, has been a vivid feeling of existing where things are on the *verge*. The verge of … something else. And it is hardly certain whether this something else is a sublime sunrise or a tropical storm, a bright future or a smoldering ruin. This probably sounds like a depressing way to inhabit a place. But it's also been a dynamic place in which to teach college, which is my occupation. Most of my students exhibit a keen sense of living in this culturally rich and ecologically fraught region.

As my colleague John Biguenet often remarks about New Orleans: "The future arrives here first." I love to walk and bicycle around New Orleans, teach my classes outside in the thick air, and watch as the city embarks on all sorts of rebuilding and city planning for the twenty-first century—including building a new airport, something that has been happening as I have been writing this book and which I discuss in some detail, in pages to come.

But there's another place that serves as my second home (or first, really). This is where I'm from in the northwest corner of lower Michigan, the Sleeping Bear Dunes National Lakeshore. My parents live there, and two of my siblings live nearby with their own families. The dunes are one part of the Leelanau Peninsula, which is the pinky finger of Michigan construed as a mitten: over 100 miles of sand dunes and lakeshore, the western side (where my home is) facing Wisconsin. After many years visiting this place in the summers as a young child, my parents spontaneously bought a small wedge of land and a house right on the edge of the national park. They moved my family up from suburban southern Michigan, and I came to know the area in a whole new way—in all seasons and weather, down the backroads and two-tracks, the textures of the tree bark, dappled light coming through the canopies, and the feel of lichen underfoot.

I return with my own family to this place in the summers, and sometimes in the winter too. It's a relatively quiet, wilderness supplement to our school-year urban life in New Orleans. I spent a sabbatical there in 2016–17, and I told some stories from that year in my book *The Work of Literature in an Age of Post-Truth*. In some ways, this book is a follow-up to that one.

I'm often homesick for this place during the school year. I long for the dunescapes and pine forests, the fern valleys and rolling meadows. For the sweeping shoreline of Lake Michigan, with all its overwhelming drama and ever-changing moods. It's this home that I'm sick for. Yet "home" has become so much more complicated, with the Anthropocene in mind. I can't honestly claim this place as any kind of removed, bracketed-off space or region. I know too well that it is a privileged realm, that the feeling of it being more natural is in fact *artificial*. But still, I long for being up in Michigan, hoping that it can serve as a point of orientation in the dizzying awareness that I am an agent of the Anthropocene.

In his recent book *Down to Earth*, Bruno Latour writes about the conundrum of how to grasp and adjust to the reality of human-caused damage incurred on a planetary scale: "Each of us thus faces the following question: Do we continue to nourish dreams of escaping, or do we start seeking a territory that we and our children can inhabit? Either we deny the existence of the problem, or else *we look for a place to land*" (5). For me, Leelanau has always been this place to land. But it has also become a more complicated location as any stable sense of the *local* has become inextricable from *global* dynamics: pollution, extreme weather patterns, hyper-consumerism, the drive to be "connected" everywhere and always, and so on.

For a long time, I wanted to write a book about this place—but it kept eluding me. I'd make inroads, jot down notes and essayettes—but then I'd get lost or find myself back where I started. I even abandoned that book at one point. Then, several years later, as I began to think more about the Anthropocene, I realized that *this* was what I had been writing about all along, as I reflected on Michigan. It's how the comforting idea of a familiar place gets uncomfortable—even haunted—as one accepts the idea that humans are laying waste to the planet, enough to affect things like species populations, rising ocean levels, and climate patterns.

I had originally been conceiving of my Michigan book as a sort of twenty-first-century *Walden*—with full knowledge and awareness of the complexities and oddities of that book, and Thoreau's rather ambiguous project of living somewhat "simply" out in the woods. I was trying to write a book about place that acknowledged the vexed history and complex landscape of North American nature writing. I was trying to write about a place I know in a way that I could derive eco-critical lessons that were translatable beyond the geographic boundaries of the place itself. I didn't want it to be merely a regional book that appealed only to those who had spent time there; I wanted it to *travel*, indeed to travel with all the baggage of contemporary life in tow. But that ended up meaning the Anthropocene, too. So what is this place? Because, now, it has found its way into *this* book—a quite different, more scattered tale.

I spent my high school years exploring the woods, lakes, shorelines, and rivers of this region: foraging for morel mushrooms, catching bass and pike in crystal clear inland lakes, and walking the lakeshore after storms sifting through assorted amalgams of plastic six-pack holders, driftwood, deflated balloons, dead minnows, beach glass, zebra mussels, firework rocket nosecones, and glacial rocks. I worked seasonal jobs in some of the dives and fancy resorts that pepper the peninsula. I return to some of these places and memories throughout the first part of this book, even though it is *not* the Michigan book I set out to write many years ago. I also reflect on new developments, observations, and experiences of the towns and cultural nodes throughout the landscape. But then, Michigan becomes just another locus amid the sprawling growth of this late North American country (and the world at large) mired in the Anthropocene.

***

The place I call home, where my parents bought a small wedge of land in 1991, sits directly on the boundary of Sleeping Bear Dunes National Lakeshore: 35 miles of sandy beaches, steep cliffs, and rolling juniper-dotted dunes that back up into pine and aspen transition zones, which then lead to deep rolling hills of maple and beech forests.

When I was in high school I watched some of my favorite hillsides get logged, cleared, and built on: gaudy luxury summer mansions thrown up double-time, echoing disjointed architectural dreams from other regions, distant coasts. Around that time, I read Edward Abbey's novel *The Monkey Wrench Gang*, and I relished fantasies of sabotaging the Caterpillar earthmovers that decimated the giant northern red oak and white ash trees.

A couple years later, at a small liberal arts college in southern Michigan, where I majored in philosophy and English, I was introduced by my professor Pete Olson to the writings of Gretel Ehrlich, Gary Snyder, and Barry Lopez, among others. I began to draw connections between bioregionalism and poetics—or how we tell stories about the places we live, and in turn how habitats and ecosystems get into the stories we tell. But one of my favorite courses in college (and easily the hardest) was a biology class called Michigan Flora—thank goodness for a strict yet open liberal arts common curriculum. There were two of us students in the class (2!), and we spent hours seeking out and identifying various species of plants, trees, and shrubs in the surrounding scrub forests and roadside ditches next to vast monoculture cornfields. I took this scientific knowledge back up north with me the following summer, and my sense of the place I called home became even more ingrained, if also overlaid with Western scientific identification practices.

Later in college I spent two summers in Wyoming, where I worked as a river guide on the Snake River within the wild, 27-mile corridor between Yellowstone and Grand Teton National Park called the J. D. Rockefeller Memorial Parkway. This was a beautiful place, but the lodgepole pines did nothing for me compared with the lusciously soft white pines back in Michigan, and the tourism industry of the American West made my woes about northern Michigan tourists seem quaint. My second summer in Wyoming, I worked a stint on a trail crew for the National Forest Service and got to know a good portion of the Bridger-Teton National Forest, clearing brush and maintaining remote trails.

After college I was drawn back to this region, in part due to my forays into the literature of the American West; I wanted to move to a mountain town. After working another river guiding job in Arizona for a season, I found my way to Bozeman, Montana, where I had been accepted into a master's program in English. When I wasn't reading for graduate seminars, working on essays, or teaching freshman writing, I fished—often with my professor and friend Greg Keeler—in the creeks and rivers that course through the Gallatin Valley and eventually form the Missouri River.

In graduate school, guided by my professors Linda Karell and Susan Kollin, my early interests in philosophy merged into critical theory, and concepts from this interdisciplinary field shaped my master's thesis, which analyzed the strange idea of "Nature" in texts ranging from Terry Tempest Williams's stark desert notes to glossy magazine advertisements for sport utility vehicles. I drew from ecofeminism, semiotics, and deconstruction in order to complicate the as-if simple ideas of landscape, environment, and region embedded in literary and cultural texts of the American West. The Anthropocene was not yet widely in the critical lexicon, but it was looming. Jedidiah Purdy's book *After Nature* captures what I was nudging toward, even though this book came out a dozen years after I lived in Bozeman: "The Anthropocene finds its most radical expression in our acknowledgement that the familiar divide between people and the natural world is no longer useful or accurate. Because we shape everything, from the upper atmosphere to the deep seas, there is no more nature that stands apart from human beings" (2).

Meanwhile, as I was working on my graduate degree and fishing the rivers, something else was happening in my life. I had taken a part-time job at the Gallatin Field Airport, eight miles outside of town, with the intention of simply making a few hundred extra bucks each month to pay my rent. But as it goes with some part-time gigs in life, I started volunteering to cover some of my coworkers' shifts, and in a matter of months I learned all the various parts of the job: loading bags, deicing the planes, emptying the onboard toilet, operating the jet bridge, pushing back the plane to the taxiway, creating itineraries for passengers, and more. Soon I was working nearly full-time at the airport, strange late and early hours that still let me keep up with my graduate studies and teaching (not to mention my fishing).

The bizarre environment and intricacies of airport life mesmerized me, including all the ways that people were syphoned in and out of this popular region of the American West via an eerily generic terminal building. I worked at the airport during and after the state-of-exception that would become known as 9/11, and I watched the norms of air travel morph and twist with the charged politics of that time. Global transit, petro-modernity, and geopolitics were getting more and more bound up and entangled with one another—and the impacts were spreading out and punctuating everyday life around the world. The Anthropocene was in the air, if not yet fully enunciated in the books I was reading or in what I was writing at the time.

When I finished my master's program I turned in my United Airlines uniform and headed West once again, this time to Davis, California, where I had been accepted into a doctoral program in English. This was *the* place to be for studying eccentric topics where nature and culture collide. At UC Davis, under the Pacific Flyway where every day the paths of migrating birds and Air Force cargo planes intermingle, I continued to study twentieth-century American literature, environmental aesthetics, and critical theory. Gary Snyder had just retired when I arrived, but his legacy was carried on by an eclectic assortment of artists and scholars.

All the while, my airport work experiences were simmering in my brain. It occurred to me somewhat gradually that I had spent lots of time in a particularly rich—if also particularly fraught—kind of *ecotone*. And I had done an ethnography without knowing it at the time.

I also started to notice weird airport scenes in a wide range of literary and cultural texts, and started to keep records of these strange instances and how they depended on notions of place, space, and environmental awareness (or not). I ended up writing my doctoral dissertation on how airports became unexpected literary environments.

The wonderful members of my dissertation committee at UC Davis influenced how I researched and wrote about airports. Caren Kaplan was working on aerial perception and militarization; Colin Milburn was researching the interpenetrations of nanotechnology and everyday life; and my dissertation director Scott Shershow taught a seminar on sovereignty and political theory that triggered an epiphany about aerial life and systems of power on the ground.

Then I worked as a research assistant for Timothy Morton as he wrote his books *Ecology without Nature* and *The Ecological Thought*. Tim's ideas about the construction of Nature with a capital "N" in literary history inspired me to ask different sorts of questions about the roles of literature, poetics, and narrative with respect to concepts of environment and transit. Tim would become one of the more important thinkers of the Anthropocene, and he became a great mentor and friend.

My dissertation formed the basis for my eventual book *The Textual Life of Airports: Reading the Culture of Flight*. I wrote this book during my first couple years at Loyola University New Orleans, where I was hired in a tenure-track position to teach contemporary literature and critical theory.

Over the next ten years at Loyola I continued to write about air travel, always coming from an oblique environmental sensibility. I wrote two more books about airports: *The End of Airports* and *Airportness: The Nature of Flight*. And throughout these years I was gradually working on my Michigan book, but it kept feeling by turns too big and too small.

My Michigan writings ventured into the iconic white pines, woodcocks, ferns, morel mushrooms, and mythical black bears of the region. But I was equally interested in tourist traps, Day-Glo raincoats, loaded Honda Odyssey minivans, jet engines, and buoy-demarcated swim areas. In writing about this naturally beautiful area, I was casting a wide net, and so I caught a lot of gaudy things along the way—so many things that a Michigan book, or even a broader book about "place," couldn't contain it. The book started to be overwhelmed by the ambiguities of the Anthropocene, the ways that borders become porous and unwieldy. The way that nothing gets let off the hook.

***

Lake Michigan is over 40 miles wide along the Leelanau Peninsula. You can't see the other side of the lake, and visitors will often remark with surprise that it looks—and feels, minus the salt—like the ocean. Large expanses of the peninsula are protected parkland, under the designation of the Sleeping Bear Dunes National Lakeshore. Other trails and swaths of forest have been acquired and are maintained by the Leelanau Conservancy. Perhaps my favorite parts of the peninsula are the dozens of glacial lakes and meandering rivers and creeks that intersperse the hills and cedar swamps.

The Leelanau Peninsula is a magical place, expansive and pristine, if also tormented by summer tourism and all the cultural pressures that come with migrant labor and seasonal economic ebbs and flows. And I am not innocent in this matrix. Each summer when I head up north with my family I continue to be amazed, humbled, and schooled by this place I still call home. This book in part accounts for some of the old and new lessons I've learned from this area—little totems of sorts that I've collected around the Leelanau Peninsula. But as I've collected them, the totems have crumbled in my hands and the pieces spilled out onto the lichen-covered soil. The ground sometimes became asphalt. A control tower sometimes appeared on the horizon. Dark gray cargo planes flew fatly overhead. What follows are notes on the Anthropocene, starting from up in Michigan then spiraling beyond.

Plenty of books have been written—and are still being written—about the Anthropocene. The idea—that human activity has made a discernible, damaging impact on the planet—has inspired disturbing works of art, trenchant philosophical investigations, rigorous scientific studies, and imaginative novels and films. In the pages that follow I write about the Anthropocene impressionistically and associatively. I track the residues and ramifications of the Anthropocene in the proximity of two topics where the concept may seem somewhat less obvious, at times—if also where it becomes all the more haunting. These are sites that are close to me, if asymmetrically so: the place I call home, up in Michigan; and air travel—a long-standing personal obsession and philosophical preoccupation. Searching for the Anthropocene around these familiar loci makes the concept both more graspable *and* more dispersing, everywhere.

Totem Shop

Some of my earliest memories are of spending the summers on the beach, especially a particular scent that lingers in the dunes just prior to where the conifers taper off and the dune grass thickens before giving way to the sand and the water. It's an aromatic admixture of juniper berries, dry sand, and pine needles, and it hovers in this nebulous zone between the white pines and the balsam poplars. Tromping down the boardwalk, hopping here and there to avoid old two-by-sixes that had sprouted splinters, I would pass through it and the odor would permeate—and that's when I'd know I was home.

Most summers when I was young, my parents would rent a house for a week or two on Sleeping Bear Bay. A stretch of residential shoreline interrupts the national park for a few miles, here, and a few dozen new and old houses are afforded perfect views and beach access. We could walk the sandy beach down the curve of the bay, watching the Manitou Islands change shape in the distance. The lake was clear and usually warm enough to swim in by late June—but almost as important, we could walk into the tourist gauntlet that is the little town of Glen Arbor.

The spot that held a special place in my imagination was a log cabin-ish store called the Totem Shop. It featured an authentic-looking totem pole on the outside and a glyph near the door of a stone-faced Indian proffering tobacco and some other mysterious objects to would-be customers. But this was no rustic trading outpost; no, this store sold Gobstoppers and Jolly Ranchers out of barrels, cheap sunglasses off a spinning rack, knives of all sizes and styles (from woodsy looking buck knives to switchblades that looked as though they'd been imported from a pawnshop in downtown Detroit), fake spears, real moccasins, raincoats, Michigan-themed T-shirts, and hundreds of other trinkets and baubles.

Down at the beach, my father would give my big sister and me a nickel for each piece of sea glass we could find and a dime for each Petoskey stone. On any given day we'd collect piles of these little gems, and then cash out sometime in the afternoon—heading into town to the Totem Shop to stock up on jawbreakers, plastic jewelry, or other junk.

I especially recall saving my beach earnings to buy a certain type of slingshot. In the corner of the store was a wood crate full of them: each slingshot was unique, constructed out of a stick in the shape of a Y and fastened to thick rubber bands knotted in each of the two upper ends. A small leather pouch joined the bands in the middle. I don't know whether it was the simplicity of design or the primitive aura, but I was transfixed by these things.

Back at the cottage I would collect small white stones off the sand and practice my shot, getting used to the pull and release of the rubber, and softening with my fingertips the leather pouch that held the projectiles. Sufficiently practiced and slingshot broken-in, I'd assemble another stash of stones and then settle into a depression in the dunes, concealed by the razor-sharp dune grass. I was waiting for the seagulls to alight close enough by—and then I would ambush and assail them with my still new handcrafted weapon from the Totem Shop. Picture a startled flock soaring up again and angling out over the surf, while I barely launched a second stone. It was a laughable scene, really—the gulls were a thousand times more adroit than I gave them credit for.

Looking back on this, I'm embarrassed that I spent these concentrated hours of my childhood hunting harmless seagulls. What attracted me to this predatory scheme, to this expression of tactical violence? Of course I know: it is part of the unconscious of the Anthropocene, the inheritance of generations of the militarization of everyday life. You think you're just an innocent boy on the beach trying to pick off abundant shorebirds—but you're implicated in it down deep. The Ojibwa myth of the Sleeping Bear belies the fact immediately: This very land was ruthlessly colonized, reparations for which have not been made.

It is common these days to find a few dead seagulls on the beach on any given morning, their wasted and wrecked bodies collapsed and washed up amid driftwood, oak leaves, balloons, firework casings, and other plastic detritus. This is the result of the type E botulism plaguing the seagulls these days. The Department of Natural Resources has official language for this disease that sounds like it could be read on a tattered sign in Cormac McCarthy's post-apocalyptic novel *The Road*: "Dead birds should not be removed from another landowner's property without permission." What kind of place is this?

Sometimes I find seagulls pecking away at dead carp and whitefish carcasses at the edge of the surf—these gulls will be future victims of the botulism, still alive but unable to fly or walk. They'll sit there on the sand looking up as you pass by, as if hoping for some reprieve or quick death. To stumble on the sick or dead gulls—as well as cormorants and merganser ducks—is to confront a gruesome range of symptoms and stages of decay. This is not the Up North that people come to see, where, again in the words of the Michigan DNR, "consciousness is retained" in spite of increasing "muscular paralysis." Or perhaps these dead and dying birds are not all that far removed from why certain places come to stand for *vacation*, at all. I once found a Frisbee on the beach that was advertising a chiropractic clinic in Glen Arbor; as the various skeletons on the beach suggest, humans share the fate of spinal columns with the birds and the fish.

The Totem Shop is still around, and in fact it looks like it's doing better than ever. Several wooden Indian statues and statuettes continue to adorn the place, if somewhat dubiously. There's a crouching warrior with a bow, and a squaw with a papoose. There's also a rather disjunctive cowboy statue, nearly human scale, with a pistol and belt full of ammunition.

The slingshots are still there, though they look surprisingly small and chintzy from my older perspective. What really strikes me now, however, is the huge wall covered with toy guns for sale. Revolver cap-guns, M-16 assault rifles, fluorescent squirt cannons, camouflage .45s, wooden eighteenth-century ball pistols—it is a veritable panoply of plastic firearms, all in the service of the pleasure and thrills of an Up North vacation.

Is this armory of play guns an odd nod to our proximity to Michigan Militia activity? Or is it some strange signifier of freedom coincident with the anarchy of summertime? It's baffling to me now, even as I can remember playing gleefully with such guns as a kid.

One afternoon while in the Totem Shop I watched two teenage boys pantomime a Hollywood-style execution with one of these guns: one boy picked up a pistol, cocked it like a professional, and leveled it with ease and steady hand at the other boy's forehead, right between the eyes. He mouthed some words (I was a foot too far away to hear what they were), and then pulled the trigger. Clack.

They guffawed and ambled over to the knife display case, proceeding to demonstrate certain jabs, upward thrusts, and rips that one could presumably perform with the blades inside.

This was late in the summer of 2012, mere weeks after the Batman movie massacre in Aurora, Colorado, when James Eagan Holmes stormed into a theater with guns and tear gas grenades, killing 12 people and injuring another 70. In the Totem Shop, under the dark shadow of this event, was the gunplay mere innocent, adolescent farce? Perhaps—but the similarities were chilling. Were there family resemblances to my own pointless childhood seagull hunting sprees? Yes, there were.

A new aspect of the Totem Shop since my childhood is the dramatic upscaling of the outdoor apparel for sale. As one example, now the Totem Shop sells Patagonia jackets and clothing, full racks displaying their bright high-performance laminates, breathable fabrics, and fashionable prints. Patagonia is a company dedicated to environmental action and ecological causes. Patagonia prides itself on supporting sustainability and ethical manufacturing. Much of their gear is made from recycled plastic, and increasingly Patagonia's clothes are recyclable, as well: you can literally send your worn-out clothes to them and they will recycle or repurpose the fabric.

To enter the world of Patagonia is to confront ecological awareness and consumerism, fickle design trends and steadily high ideals, wish images of a purer world alongside the toxic maelstrom of global tourism. It is not only dazzling adventure vacations and athletic human bodies but also complex political-economic arrangements and quagmires concerning globalization and containerization. Patagonia is a site where all these messy vectors collide—and as such, it is an Anthropocenic object lesson.

Anthropologist Anna Tsing writes of the Anthropocene, "the term is still new—and still full of promising contradictions" (19). I stand in the Totem Shop and turn around, looking at the high-end outdoor gear, the vast toy gun rack, the handmade slingshots, and carved Indian figures … and I wonder. What is this shop where Native American iconography, plastic imitation weaponized violence, and ecologically attuned adventure gear confusingly converge? It's far north in a vacation wonderland, but also in the pit of the Anthropocene. This collection of totems conjures all of this place, in miniature. It is a site of role-play and real adventure, of coexisting species and mortal combat. This store holds all the promises of an escape and many reminders of that which cannot be left behind.

Trash Shock

One late summer day, probably in 1995, my mother dropped me off in Leland, seven miles north of our home, while she went to work at the library. I took the long walk back, around Whaleback Point and past eroding dunes and beachside mansions.

I didn't have a purpose for this walk other than to simply do it; I had driven this expanse on the road above the shore countless times, but I had never walked the length from Leland to home, on the beach. The beginning area was entirely new territory: break walls and beach access boardwalks that lead up to cottages, or sometimes huge estates. There's even a house rumored to have belonged to Al Capone, replete with a gun turret and the piers of a private dock still visible in the water.

As I walked, I noticed amalgams of plastic trash washed into miniature coves and heaped among zebra mussel shells and stones. I had worn my backpack (mostly empty) for some reason, and I began to put things into my pack as I walked. Sometimes the items were tiny plastic pieces: pull-tabs from juice packs, cap locks from soda bottles, broken off parts of toys, go cups, and drinking straws—so many drinking straws. Other times, I'd find an entire yellow motor oil container or a plastic pallet (like the kind used in bread delivery trucks). Frayed nylon rope, plastic shovels for beach play, splayed shot cups from shotgun shells, six-pack holders, indecipherable plastic shards, snapped off … something. All this I stuffed into my bag, to the point where I had no room left, and I then started to strap things to the outside of the pack, using the straps and loops intended for climbing gear.

Nearing the public beach at the northern end of the National Lakeshore, where I turn up toward my home, I realized that people on the beach were fleeing toward the parking lot as they saw me coming. I paused, and realized what I looked like: some sort of post-apocalyptic roving salvager, like one of the trash pickers from Jim Henson's *Labyrinth*, an enormous mound of garbage on my back, heading toward the civilized vacation beach.

It was funny to me, then. But the mass collected from just a few hours of walking on the beach also shocked something in me, a recognition of the patterns of consumption and waste. Patterns that I was implicated in, even as I was picking up after them. Barely making a dent, of course. The next big storm would dump thousands of pounds of new micro- and macro-plastics on the shores of Lake Michigan.

Over twenty years later, when I spent the winter in Michigan during my sabbatical, I took regular walks on the beach, always picking up whatever trash I could find—collecting it and often photographing it, trying to make some sense of it (while also risking aestheticizing it, by tweeting it). It is becoming well known that human-produced plastic refuse is amassing in the oceans, and increasingly laying waste to myriad species that cannot avoid ingesting this detritus. If plastics are created for better (human) living, we now know that this kind of living takes a toll on our vaster lifeworld. As the editors of the book *Arts of Living on a Damaged Planet* put it, "The ecological simplifications of the modern world—products of the abhorrence of monsters—have turned monstrosity back against us, conjuring new threats to livability" (M6). I am a monster, finding the traces of monstrous life on the beach.

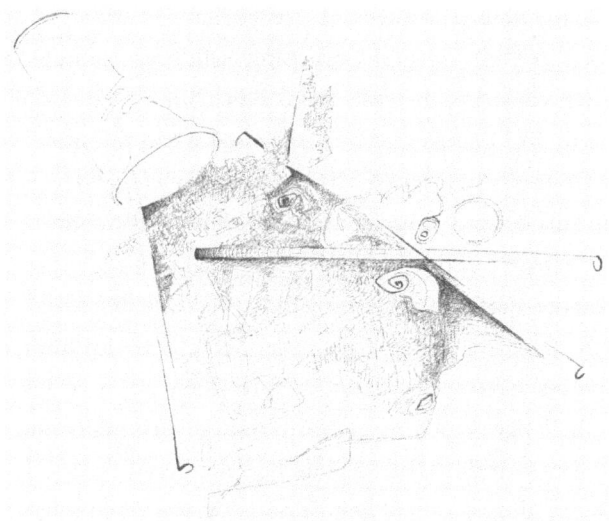

Figure 2 *Drawing lesson: Anthropocene amalgam. Illustration by Lara Schaberg.*

Disenchantment and all, these beach walks are nevertheless beautiful, *and* they open up the mind to vaster scales of space and time—spans that make even the progress of humankind appear as a blip, pollution and all. But this is hardly meant to excuse human cycles of production and excretion. The shock of trash juxtaposed with the sublimity of the beach poses a question, to me: What might it mean to take this kind of double awareness seriously, to reassess the plastic filth and adjust our modes of living, while also appreciating the relative, imminent oblivion of our species?

Whose World

It's looming out there, the Anthropocene. I can smell it in the oily air that settles over my home city of New Orleans, and I can see it in the yellow Dollar General bags scattered on the ground every morning in front of my house. Further out, everywhere: erratic storms, species extinction, coastal erosion, sweeping wildfires, polluted waters, melting ice caps. Beach trash freezes in chunky ice sheets on the shoreline up in Michigan, to be discovered when the snow melts. As William Connolly puts it in his book *Facing the Planetary*, "A tiger has us by the tail; we are swinging around without really coming to terms with the character of the Anthropocene" (184).

Still, on the day that I am writing this, a *Wall Street Journal* article by Greg Ip declares that things have never been better for humans in all of our species' history, and that therefore surely we can overcome our current challenges, such as authoritarian governments and climate change ("The World Is Getting Quietly, Relentlessly Better," January 2, 2019). But in Ip's assessment lies the paradox: the very things that have improved human life in general, or for part of the population, have hastened and intensified the negative impact of human activity on the planet—thereby shortening our potential time here. For instance, the roar overhead right now: that's a mundane commercial airliner leaving Louis Armstrong International, spewing kerosene fuel exhaust and networked into thousands of other simultaneous flights around the globe. Air travel is a vast machine of human mobility, its fumes and forms at once ephemeral and always accumulating, punishment confused for progress.

I have been searching for the Anthropocene for many years. But I've been *in* it for even longer—really, my whole life. This predicament sums up the effort (and the quandary) of my book: trying to locate, delineate, and understand something that I'm also enmeshed with at every turn, and which I dragged around with me for years before becoming aware of it. The Anthropocene is an overwhelming topic to think about, partly because it implicates the thinker. But also because, in the words of environmental scientist Erle Ellis, the Anthropocene "demands action" (143). But just what sort of action?

From whom, exactly? How soon? On what scale? And to what end? All these questions can fluster, and paralyze. So much easier to retreat to comfortable habits and familiar patterns of life. And so the Anthropocene recedes into the murky background, for now.

What would it mean to keep the idea of the Anthropocene at the level of consciousness?

There's a MacGyver episode from 1985, called "Trumbo's World," that serves as an example of how I search for the Anthropocene and how I find it in unexpected places. This one I found while introducing my 8-year-old son Julien to the character of MacGyver (admittedly a questionable parenting choice).

The story of this episode hinges on an ecological mystery in a South American jungle, where birds are fleeing their natural habitat at an alarming rate. Under the pretext of urgent scientific research, MacGyver heads to the jungle with an ornithologist friend named Charlie. Far up the river (there is a whiff of *Heart of Darkness* here) the two of them encounter a "lawless," gun-toting man named Trumbo, who has "beaten back" the wild land to create a small empire: a cacao plantation and dozens of indentured laborers who toil under Trumbo's severe rule. Trumbo touts his self-made paradise, and MacGyver seems by turns slightly amused and sincerely impressed. It turns out that a colony of soldier ants has erupted in the jungle nearby; they are swarming and devouring everything in their path. Upon discovering the roving carpet of insects, Charlie is mesmerized and starts taking pictures of the ants for documentation—only to be suddenly swarmed, himself. Charlie slips and falls, and is almost immediately consumed by the ants and killed. MacGyver couldn't get to Charlie in time to save his friend. Pandemonium breaks out on the plantation, and the workers quickly head to the river to flee, as Trumbo enjoins them to stay and fight, and even threatens them with a shotgun—whereupon MacGyver tackles Trumbo, throws the rifle into the river, and then battles Trumbo until the workers are safely away and the two fighters tire.

Trumbo wants to stay and fight the ants. The only ones left now are Trumbo, his closest servant Luiz, and MacGyver—who, confoundingly, offers to stay and help Trumbo. They come up with a plan to flood the cacao fields and wash away the ants; when this partially fails and Luiz is overtaken by the ants, MacGyver devises a backup strategy involving a homemade flamethrower to drive away the onrushing tide of insects. This works until Trumbo's supply of gasoline runs out. Finally, MacGyver constructs a makeshift bomb and an ant-proof suit and dashes across the ant-covered expanse of land, at last blowing up the dam and flooding the plantation. MacGyver climbs out of the flooded plain and limps back, remarking with dry humor, "What a mess!" Trumbo exclaims, "Who cares, we won! I'll build it again … better this time!" In the closing moments of the episode, MacGyver and Trumbo saunter back into the walled-in estate, bantering like old pals.

The implications of this episode are mind-boggling. What begins as an ecological mystery in need of objective scientific understanding gets converted into a ridiculous man-against-Nature narrative, and MacGyver ends up befriending the rugged individualist Trumbo. Charlie the scientist friend and Luiz the loyal slave are both killed off with barely any emotional register—and there are no ethical takeaways to speak of, for the viewer. This is atypical of MacGyver, whose episodes tend to proffer basic lessons in liberal morality and secular ethical behavior. Instead, the episode is like a MacGyver fever dream: problem-solving begets problem-solving, but in such a way that any "big picture" is lost.

"Trumbo's World" exhibits something disturbing about searching for the Anthropocene: it's in the way the story continually seems to forget what it is about, or who or what is important and significant in the story. Is it a lesson in learning about and respecting ecosystems? Or about recognizing exploitative systems so as to change them? Or about surviving the brute force of Nature at any cost? About the importance of loyalty and friendship, or about the core value of self-interest? Is it about communing with a vast interconnected world, or about a rotting nihilism that drives human enterprise? The contradictions within and between these questions—and the impossibility of determining whether or not any of these questions become paramount, not to mention settled—drive "Trumbo's World."

Another reason "Trumbo's World" struck me as pertinent to the Anthropocene is because of the ways that ecological catastrophe is first recognized as a critical focal point of the episode only to be quickly corralled into a human-centric problem, a problem that is "solved" in a bizarrely limited and temporary sense. The soldier ants are totally washed away, and so plantation life can recommence—along with all the pernicious economic structures necessary for this way of life to thrive. The Anthropocene in this episode is isolated neither in the agricultural control of the landscape nor in the simplistic understanding (and blunt treatment) of the soldier ants. Rather, the Anthropocene descends on this episode as a contagious sort of myopia: everyone is terribly near-sighted, to a fault. It is telling that the episode ends with MacGyver receding into the plantation, as if Trumbo's newly found henchman. Of course, MacGyver was always just hired help called in by some centralized power holders. Throughout the early seasons of the show, MacGyver often tries to get out into the wilderness, which he claims to love so much—to simply go camping or fishing or hang-gliding—but he is always sucked back into strange work to take care of chemical spills, hijackings, cases of international espionage, or a lurking nemesis. The Anthropocene always strikes back: it is the relentless, unshakable problem that is only exacerbated by attempts to escape or solve any single dilemma at hand.

MacGyver's is a fictional "world" that nevertheless ends up feeling all too similar to our contemporary Anthropocene conundrum, because it is understood to be *possessed* from the outset: *Trumbo's* world, *our* world. Acknowledging the Anthropocene is one step toward recognizing this problem. But the search for its textures and contours, its causes and solutions, becomes no less difficult upon recognition. As Bruno Latour explains the challenge,

> We must face up to what is literally a problem of dimension, scale, and lodging: the planet is *much too narrow and limited* for the globe of globalization; at the same time, it is *too big*, infinitely too large, to active, too complex, to remain within the narrow and limited borders of any locality whatsoever. We are all overwhelmed twice over: by what is too big, and by what is too small. (*Down to Earth*, 16)

My home up in Michigan has posed this exact problem for me, feeling by turns vast and microcosmic, globally enmeshed and provincial, at once. But it's what I have to work with, and it makes real some of the more abstract implications and entanglements of the Anthropocene.

Abandoned Resort, Active Airfield

In his book *Ecocriticism on the Edge*, Timothy Clark observes how the Anthropocene "forms an indeterminate but insidious threshold at which many actions previously normal or insignificant have become, often in all innocence, themselves destructive, simply by virtue of human numbers and power" (61). In Michigan I find myself continually residing in such a vague space, dawdling on an unclear line. To find footing in the place I call home, even as I lose my bearing along the way.

Back when I was in college, when I'd be home for winter break I would work at the nearby ski resort as a lift operator. It was a relatively easy way to make a few hundred bucks in between semesters, money to buy books with when I returned to school a couple weeks later. But they were long cold days sitting in a shack at the top of the "mountain" (elevation: 1,100 feet), watching skiers in bright suits file past and occasionally stopping the lift to untangle someone's equipment from a chair or extricate a dragged child.

I remember one day the wind became too fierce and we couldn't run the lifts, but we were required to stay at our stations in the event that the wind died down; the skiers were waiting in the lodge drinking hot chocolates and hot toddies, eager to use their new goggles and gloves. That day I sat in the shack at the top of the hill and read Jack Kerouac's *Big Sur* for the first time, thrilled by the somewhat parallel experience of feeling alone while totally entrenched in a weird cultural zone.

Now the resort is closed, the old red lift cables drooping, gear houses overgrown around the hill. I drove up to the resort one July afternoon because I wanted to see the landing strip; there's an airfield next to the hill that is still in use.

I parked the car and walked over to the field. A tiny, outhouse-size structure stood in the grass with a very small sign on it: AIRPORT. There was an old phone inside, and that was all. A few small propeller planes were tied down to the ground on a grassy field next to the asphalt runway. No business jets were in sight; they tend to fly in, drop off mysterious passengers and then roar off again, private aircraft or commoditized NetJets on to other lucrative routes.

But on this day I didn't expect to be taken with the sight of the defunct resort. The hotel with its creepy dark windows and heavy curtains drawn, and the columns of the grand entrance I used to pass through on the way to the lift operators' break room (more of a closet with a permanent micro-plume of marijuana smoke lingering by the ceiling panels), where our uniform parkas hung and where we punched in and out of our shifts. I was caught in a sudden trance, barraged with memories and residual sense perceptions. I turned back to the planes, but the eerie feeling stayed with me.

While the airstrip is still in use, it isn't monitored by a control tower; aircraft simply communicate with one another to make sure no one is in the way when a landing or takeoff is imminent. It's a very short runway, and I'm often startled by the size of some of the planes cruising in for landing as they arc in over my parents' home a couple miles away.

After snapping a few pictures of the motley gang of planes, I was drawn back to the parking lot and I just stared at the derelict assemblage of buildings. Every time I'm back home I hear things about the resort and read angry letters to the editor in the local paper, calling for its demolition or rehabilitation. There was one time when it was rumored to have been bought by a wealthy Scientologist; the resort would become one of those infamous compounds where celebrities are secreted away and forcibly detoxed and reeducated. And who knows? Maybe it is. That would certainly explain the business jets that swoop in and scream off again periodically, extraordinary renditions of the rich and famous. But then there was some Las Vegas mogul slated to buy it, to turn it into a world-class snowboard park. The deal fell through due to a scandal of one kind or another. Small communities thrive on such tantalizing tales and unresolved landscapes. Thus the Anthropocene sneaks into distant regions, through the stains of economic high jinx and hidden fortunes.

The hill itself is actually a natural topographical feature, one of the highest points in the county where I'm from—making it unlike other terraformed ski resorts of the Midwest, where people play on sculpted piles of dirt or trash. I've always thought it would be nice to see the hill reabsorbed by the surrounding terrain: first sumac, creeping junipers, and wild grape vines, then gradually pines and oaks, and then the huge beech and maple trees that make up the climax forests of the region. It will happen eventually, one way or another. Unless other essential ecosystem components are compromised, as tick populations rise and fauna try to adjust accordingly.

I'm writing this early in the morning, as the sky changes from the darkest purple to a faintly glowing slate gray. Innumerable birds are sounding off in the woods, reminding me of other beings in flight. Somewhere, a private plane is likely filing a flight plan that involves a landing at the airstrip by the ski hill, and the abandoned resort will wait for their arrival.

How do we get from the woods of a protected national lakeshore to the dispersed textual life of air travel and beyond? Through the branching tunnel of the Anthropocene. Sometimes this tunnel looks verdant and viney, and other times it looks like a steel culvert or a cement underpass. All the passages connect, yet it is never immediately clear just how and where, or when.

Logging Camp

During Julien's second year on this planet, we enjoyed reading Richard Scarry's classic book *Cars and Trucks and Things That Go*. I was revisiting this book, myself—it was uncanny how vividly I remembered some of the scenes, as I hadn't seen the pages in thirty years or so.

In Scarry's animated world, it turns out that pretty much everything *goes*, and everything has a perspective—even nonliving things. The book could be understood as a primer to Object-Oriented Ontology, or the philosophy that holds, as Ian Bogost summarized it pithily on his website once, "that nothing has special status, but that everything exists equally." A scene that kept catching Julien's fascination early on were the pages where the pig family (the road-tripping main characters of the story) passes a logging camp. Scarry depicted a razed landscape, shorn tree trunks being hauled across the eerie white background of the page. A team of anthropomorphized cats, pigs, and raccoons operate heavy machinery by way of dispatching the logs. A pink outhouse trailer sits at the edge of the no longer forest.

These pages turned out to provide a useful, if unexpected, education of sorts. The following summer up in Michigan people were logging the woods behind my family's house, on a piece of land in the conservancy. The near constant buzzing of the STIHL chainsaws mixed with intermittent cicada sirens in the trees. Each time a tree fell, the booming crash cascaded down the hillsides, strangely amplified and muffled at the same time, and practically shaking the ground underfoot for an elusive moment.

They dragged the felled trees through the woods along a fresh path that showed the gouges of the tremendous logs, with surprising glacial rocks and yellow beach sand churned up in the process. What used to be my favorite valley of waist-high bracken ferns became a staging area where the huge logs were cut into eight-foot lengths, to be hauled out on truck trailer.

I used to climb these trees—some of these exact trees. My brother and I would take a compound bow and an arrow with a lead line attached, and one of us would shoot the arrow up into the highest branches of a giant oak or beech. Then we'd pull a static climbing rope up and over, nestling it into a firm branch fork. With a climbing ascender attached to a harness, and another beneath with webbing for foot loops, we could go vertically straight into the upper canopy of the forest, fifty or sixty feet above. And then just … hang out. There is a whole other life world in the upper story of a deciduous forest. Different birds and bugs, different sounds and smells, and the ways the leaves would move around in rustling undulations, catching different currents. Nothing like a different life world to disrupt the general, day-to-day myopia of being a pilot of the Anthropocene.

I hadn't climbed trees like that in probably twenty years, but I could recall the feeling intensely. Now I was seeing some of these very trees lying on the ground, their upper branches shattered and scattered around—useless, because worthless. Tangles of discarded biomass left behind in the wake of the destruction. It was sad, and more than a little depressing.

I'm not simply waxing nostalgic. In the moment, I was actually attempting to be enchanted by the spectacle and the tremendous effort that goes into logging a forest, visibly imprinted as it is in the incredible tire tracks made by the Timberjack skidders.

And this was hardly clear-cut logging. What happened in the woods was selective logging—one might even call it *sustainable*. We need to bracket that word "sustainable," though, as it begs uncomfortable questions concerning for how long, and for whom or what purpose—especially in the temporal whorl of the Anthropocene.

The logging that happened here is fairly targeted, mostly thinning out the white ash and northern red oak trees and thus making room for new growth—the millions of seedlings and saplings sprouting up from the floor below, but which struggle to get light when the canopy is too dense. You wouldn't believe how dark it can be in the middle of the day in the thickest parts of these woods. After the loggers had moved through and done their work, there were bright splotches of sunlight on the forest floor, jagged puzzle pieces flickering on the undergrowth. The effect was disorientating and strange.

I'll admit that there was a latent part of me that drifted toward ecoterrorism, as I crept through the woods spying on the logging activities. I sort of wanted to sabotage the whole operation. Yet

I restrained myself, and instead just observed the outfit from afar, perched on an adjacent ridge. In the distance I could glimpse one of the skidders, an orange one, crashing through the trees.

In the canon of wilderness writing Gary Snyder reflected on this type of scene in the section "Logging" from his book *Myths & Texts*. Here, Snyder dutifully lists the various goings-on around an active logging camp:

> The D8 tears through piss-fir,
> Scrapes the seed-pine
> chipmunks flee,
> A black ant carries an egg
> Aimlessly from the battered ground.
> Yellowjackets swarm and circle
> Above the crushed dead log, their home.
> Pitch oozes from barked
> trees still standing,
> Mashed bushes make strange smells.
> Lodgepole pines are brittle.
> Camprobbers flutter to watch.

Rereading this section having been out in the logged woods, I recognize new details. Each line has multiple objects interacting, violently or just barely, or passing by one another oblivious ... and the human becomes one thing among many in this scene.

When Snyder notices that "mashed bushes make strange smells" it's as if the bushes are making the smells not just for the humans, but for the very strangeness of the smells themselves. I've felt this in the forest over the past few weeks: The smell of the cut trees is so pungent that it jerks me out of my own nose—I feel thrust into the underbrush, into an alien world. Likewise, in Snyder's evocation of the brittleness of the lodgepoles and the watching of the camprobbers (or gray jays), these things happen on their own trajectories, intersecting with the logging operation but also entirely of their own being. Snyder's lines might at first sound sad about the shorn forest, but the more you read of this poem, the more other entities emerge and rise up to an equal status alongside the loggers—even in the midst of the apparently human-caused turmoil.

It's not just a logging camp; it's kind of campy, too, in the sense that Susan Sontag might have described it. As Sontag writes, "I am strongly drawn to Camp, and almost as strongly offended by it. That is why I want to talk about it, and why I can." The mythology of northern Michigan also involves the prevalence of *camps*: summer camps, hunting camps, fishing camps, and so on. Camps here are contrived contexts, bracketed zones for leisure or adventure; as such, they appear as markers of Anthropocene consciousness, as if certain spaces and times can be so easily compartmentalized, set apart from the rest of "life." And yet for Sontag, "an important element of the Camp sensibility [is] the equivalence of all objects … ." This is so in Scarry's children's books, where everything comes to life—and also here in Michigan.

As hard as it is to watch, and as destructive as it seems, this logging is good for the forest in the sense that it spurs regeneration and new growth. When I told a biologist neighbor of ours about the logging, he said, "What would be *really* great would be if they burned it all down to the ground back there—then you'd *really* see some exciting species return to the area!" He's of course right. Forests thrive on dramatic upheavals and wholesale razing. It often happens on longer timescales than we can imagine or come to terms with, but to quote Sontag once again, "Camp is the attempt to do something extraordinary." The logging camp—and the forest at large, a domain without bounds, commingling with tractors and chainsaws—is indeed an attempt at something extraordinary.

The Anthropocene is not about seeing the forest for the trees, but rather realizing that neither *forests* nor *trees* start or end "somewhere" at all. You can't ever get close enough to see *a tree*, not far enough away to see *a forest*. What you're seeing is *you seeing*—inescapably part of the picture.

Poison Ivy

The worst part of poison ivy is not knowing if you have it, but thinking you might. Poison ivy is like an object correlative of awareness of living in, and being part of, the Anthropocene.

The nights extend when you notice an itching coming from (maybe) the same part of the body, repeatedly. Then the mind wanders back to the beaver pond that you hiked to earlier that day, a remote pool of water surrounded by dead cedars and wild grapevines as thick as your wrist. You went there to fly-fish and were so focused on your backcast, and not getting hung-up in the upper canopy of leaves, that you didn't notice the mass of *Toxicodendron radicans* that you'd stepped into— not until you were stripping your piled-up fly line and saw the line snap the stems which spurted their milky juices, the toxic urushiol that stains black on clothes when heated up in the washing machine. Yes, it was there on the ground, then on your line, then on your hands, then—well, then anywhere is possible.

And now here you are at 1:42 in the morning, trying to stay still so as not to rustle the covers and wake your lightly sleeping toddler across the cabin, not to mention your partner in bed next to you, and meanwhile itching terribly all around your waist. You can envision the trail of red dots starting to puff up, and you wish it were morning so you could take a shower with harsh Dial soap and dry out the rash. That's when another series of itches occur, down by your ankles.

Maybe just mosquito bites? Anything would be better than the poison ivy, which last summer got you so bad that one of your thighs inflated to the diameter and tautness of a volleyball. Even the hornets that you stumbled into last week while collecting wild blackberries, and for which you received four nasty stings—even those are preferable, they hurt bad and then they just leave you feeling slightly euphoric and numb. But the poison ivy gets in your head. Especially at night. It makes for long hours wondering if you got it, how bad, how isolated or running rampant across your skin—and when and where exactly did you get it? Were you with any of your crew, did they get it too? It's itching again, somewhere new. It could be the worst yet. Or it could be nothing. But probably it's poison ivy. And you're going to have to live with it for the next week or so.

How is this an allegory for the Anthropocene? It's a lesson for how to live with more attention to the world right outside that doesn't privilege human existence. It's a lesson about accepting inconveniences and allergens and living with them—surviving, even while the world looms larger because it's also smaller, on the inside too.

Getting Lost

One July day in 2011 I got lost in the woods, somewhere in a remote quadrant of the national lakeshore, a dense forest of tall beech and maple trees. And I mean really, really lost: totally disoriented, middle-of-the-day sun overhead and so no bearing on cardinal directions, going in meandering circles up ridges and down valleys, tromping through heavy undergrowth, wading through nearly impenetrable expanses of ferns up to my thighs, over a bog whose entire mass jiggled underfoot, through wild raspberry patches and odd groves of balsam poplars ... trying to find an elusive logging road that finally appeared right in front of me after wandering along a winding ridgeline for a mile or so.

What was supposed to be a relatively short walk in the forest, through a maidenhair fern valley and then to a somewhat remote glacial kettle lake, turned into a four-hour excursion that entailed a lot of displacement and attendant uncanny feelings of total isolation amid the old-growth deciduous forests. The tiniest details—the maidenhair fern rachis, a splotch of slime mold on a downed birch tree, *Drosera* carnivorous plants around stunted cedar tree bases, the texture of leatherwood bark—all of it took on an incredible *thingness* in the dark and circular woods. I was a mere mortal, trying to find my way back to my car amid entities much more important than me.

The weird thing is that when I got home and charted where I had been, on Google Earth, the area looked so small and easily navigable. Yet while aerial perspective and satellite imaging can certainly zoom in and out impressively and cover a lot of ground, it is very difficult to map or otherwise render the experience of getting lost. The Anthropocene was poignant to me in that moment, the possibility of the God's-eye view of satellite vision comingling with the residues of a palpable sense of total existential aloneness, profound insignificance. I realized in that moment the fantasy of total knowledge technologically proffered from above and the starkly limited realities of life on the terrestrial ground.

"I like maps, because they lie. / Because they give no access to the vicious truth" (433). So writes the poet Wislawa Szymborska. Life in the Anthropocene defies easy or total mapping; but we also must use maps to get around and to acquire *partial* views—glimpses that may shift our thinking in relation to the "vicious truth" of being earthbound creatures.

Last time I went out to those woods I got turned around almost immediately, again. What started out as a clear route quickly faded into a thousand possible deer trails, mouse paths, weird wind currents, and deceptive tree lines. I turned around and went back to my car while I still knew where I was. I drove home. I left this mystery place as it was.

Beyond Green

In the summer of 2013 I flew from Traverse City to Kansas City to attend a conference for the Association for the Study of Literature and Environment. The airport that serves Kansas City is a terminal that I would think about more a few years later, as they undertook a massive renovation project and I participated in a radio program about the merits and blind spots of airport planning. But I wasn't really tuned in to these things in 2013. I was just there for the conference, where I reconnected with old friends and met new friends who would become very important to me.

I was particularly inspired by a panel hosted by Jeffrey Jerome Cohen, whose book *Prismatic Ecology* was in the works at the time. The premise of this book is that each contributor took a color other than green and thought ecologically with it—to de-verdant, as it were, our default understandings of nature writing and eco-criticism.

On my return flights to Michigan I found myself thinking about this panel and the wonderfully child-like constraint of the project. Back up north, the next morning I went for a walk through the woods in the national lakeshore, keeping an eye out for prismatic ecologies. I took this idea in an almost ridiculously basic and literal way, walking among trees and ferns and then writing about what I perceived—but adjusting the focus away from green. It was just an experiment, but it blew my mind and reorganized the forest around me. I was able to bracket one of the default modes of Anthropocene myopia: the assumption of a nature out there that is first and foremost, or ultimately, leafy and fecund.

As I walked along a familiar trail back toward the hills, the first thing I noticed was how the newly emerging sugar maple leaves in a grove of saplings were a brilliant pink against the more mature, kelly green growth elsewhere on the trees. I was just twenty yards from the house, and already I was confronted with the fact that, as Cohen had put it, "you can't totalize green into a single system"—the tiny pink leaves in June were reminders of the late spring, and they called attention to other seasonal processes and things that resisted static coloration or even neat timing.

I found myself looking around and zooming in and out, from the weird speckled gray glacial stones under my feet to the almost glowing maroon buds at the tips of the white spruce branches. Indeed, I found that, in Cohen's words, "rainbows are perspectival": the spectrum made me take on different perspectives and adjust phenomenological registers accordingly, constantly. Considering the maroon buds on these spruce trees, I recalled how Lowell Duckert had offered the counterintuitive insight that "the color maroon is never alone." Even as I was isolating the buds and taking note of their color, which I'd never before noticed, I was given over to the realization, in Duckert's stirring words, that I was not "marooned from things, but always co-implicated with them." I found myself wondering if the white spruce was a native species (turns out it is) and recalling my own thwarted efforts as a kid to climb up one to retrieve an errant Frisbee: their branches become an impossibly thick matrix, the needles incredibly prickly, and the sap gets on everything. I have muscle memory of my thoroughly scratched teenage body, sticky with denim-destroying sap. (I would learn only much later in life that a few drops of olive oil is by far the best way to remove such sap.)

Further along the trail, I passed through a sumac stand, an aspen copse, and then entered the darker climax stage forest. Among the maples and beeches, I paused to look at the decaying stump of an old bigtooth aspen tree. The tawny brown chunks seemed simultaneously to be stacked intricately and falling randomly onto the ground. It was true, as Steve Mentz had pointed out, that "brown is a connective color—but it can stain, too." The decomposing aspen stump was indicative of the shifting stages of succession here, how the shoreline along Lake Michigan gradually changes from dune grass to junipers to pines to oaks … on and on, working through species and working them back into the soil, one day probably to be engulfed by vast glaciers again. The stump was an exception to the other trees and evidence of another logic at work. I was reminded of Mentz's open question: "What happens when blue turns to brown?"—which I took to stand for any number of slow or sudden transitions when ecosystems shift and events rupture what we thought things were *supposed* to look like. It's importantly mind-boggling and humbling to realize that such transitions are *always* taking place. If the Anthropocene is a useful concept, it may be paradoxically so: to serve as a reminder of such ongoing transition, even as it seeks to name a fairly inertial trajectory of impact so that we might transit in another direction, ourselves. What shade of brown do we want to be, when all is said and done? For whom do brown stages of decay matter, and along what timelines?

Next I entered a wide valley, a place where bracken ferns used to grow up as high as my waist, so dense that lying down under them was like downsizing and suddenly being in a miniature forest itself. We used to play hide-and-seek here as kids, one of us standing among the ferns closing our eyes, the others crawling beneath the dense canopy then freezing beneath, invisible from above. Now this valley is flattened and covered with deep tread marks—it is the site of the logging extravaganza that I wrote about earlier.

As I walked along this small wasteland, bracken fern fiddleheads just beginning to reclaim the space, I spotted a smooth blue stone, and I knelt down to look more closely at some rust-colored scratches on the stone: scrapes from the giant log skidder, probably, as it rolled through the valley dragging giant white ash, sugar maple, and red oak trunks. And this blue stone sent me back to Eileen Joy's provocative segment of the panel, about a "blues ecology": compartments such as depression, sadness, and melancholy and how these things too must be figured into ecological awareness. Joy posed the question, "Do these only take place inside one? Or are they also *in the world, atmospheric*?" My complicated feelings about the aftermath of the logging operation in the woods spoke to this problem, and the blue stone at my feet became a scarred object correlative.

Another contributor to *Prismatic Ecology*, Vin Nardizzi was not able to make it to the conference, but I had been lucky enough (thanks to my colleague Hillary Eklund) to have heard him speak at Loyola earlier that year from his chapter-in-progress. Nardizzi was interested in when ecosystems tarry with monstrosity and manufactured hybridity to the point that green becomes even *greener*. Pesticides and preservatives can keep things unnaturally green, greener than they would be otherwise; humans become the arbiter of green, but always at the severe risk of what allows for any green at all. Sometimes when I'm here in Michigan, even in the relatively *un*contaminated woods, I become overwhelmed by this sensation where nothing seems outwardly wrong, but the forest looms around me and reminds me that I am both in it and outside it, a conscious mapper of species, obeying or sneaking across property lines, going down trails, creating paths: another mere mammal passing through, yet a mammal with a disproportionate impact. This awareness, I think, is critical to recognizing and tarrying with the Anthropocene. Yet it's a feeling that can also render one helpless—because we're always greener than we think.

The Anthropocene crops up in all sorts of disciplines and comes out of divergent fields. Sometimes I feel ill-equipped or like an imposter, writing about environmental awareness from my arguably squishy humanities standpoint. In 2013 *Prismatic Ecology* stood out to me as impressively exploding how literary theorists could write about environment in the Anthropocene, using this disarmingly simple rubric. In the pages here, I am attempting a foray around this topic that is by turns emplaced and displaced, literary and cultural. My patchwork approach is a method of working with the Anthropocene as an imperfect concept, but one rife with possibilities, even aesthetic possibilities—recognizing that aestheticizing the Anthropocene may be part of the problem. I don't want to decry or simply avoid the Anthropocene; but I also resist solidifying it as if it is ever clear and distinct. The form of this book is meant to interrupt any smooth flow, while still proceeding toward a delta of sorts, or circling around a prism that changes color, expands and contracts, at each turn.

On the Water

Deep in the woods, up high enough on certain hillsides, I can look out through the trees and see a little sliver of the big lake: Lake Michigan just sitting out there, vast, wide, color banded where the green sandy shallows drop off to midnight blue, innumerable whitecaps moving on the horizon, miles offshore. Other times glassy surface extending to a sharp edge of the world.

One night as I fished the north shoreline of my favorite lake, wading up to my waist and casting a small frog pattern fly into the weeds, I heard a thunderstorm make its way over the lake. When I started out that evening, at about 7:45, it was sunny and looked to be settling in for a crystal-clear sunset. I cast into the shallows and entice several enormous fish into striking. I land a few largemouth bass, and several other fish explode out of the water in pursuit, sometimes slicing right through my line as they attempt to intercept my fly—these are toothy northern pike. Fly-fishing these lakes is as much fun as any trout fishing I ever did in Montana; though, to be honest, it isn't a fair comparison—both have their own magic, their own rhythms.

A deer came down to the shore to drink, saw me and bounded away, hooves sucking in the silty muck. I heard a dog barking in the woods—oddly, as this was in the middle of the lakeshore, no trails to speak of on that hillside—but then the barks turned into yips and howls, many at once, and I realized they were coyotes. By about 9:00, as dusk settled over the lake and as the water became mirror-like, a gray bank of clouds appeared as if out of nowhere, and I began to hear deep rumblings of distant thunder. By the time I was wading back to where I parked, rain began to fall, disturbing the still water and obscuring my sense of distance.

When I fish another of my favorite small remote lakes in the park, one very close to the big lake, I can sometimes hear the North Manitou Shoal lighthouse in the distance, its monotone foghorn sounding once every minute or so. Occasionally a freighter passes by while I'm fishing, and while I cannot see it through the dense trees, I can almost feel the throb of the huge engines, the giant propellers churning the big water.

I fish and canoe the small inland lakes, but always with an awareness of the big lake in the distance, at rest or in turmoil, usually somewhere in between. It's always there. Hemingway notes the big lake in passing in many of his Michigan stories: it's an entity at turns imposing and reassuring, dangerous and calming, mysterious and clarifying.

There are always multiple water rescues each summer, up here. The big lake is *big* and can go from glassy calm to six-foot swells in a matter of minutes, if the wind direction shifts just slightly. The new craze for paddleboards along the coasts and in the resort towns seems to have promoted a false sense of security on the lake, as if these picturesque northern bays should naturally behave like tropical coves: warm, languid, and predictable. But they don't, and no matter how expensive your board is, and no matter how hip your sunglasses and stylish your swimsuit, the water is very, very cold and you won't last long once you are tossed into it, even if you're a confident swimmer.

Frankly, I'm terrified of the big lake. I always have been. When I was 7 or 8, while at summer camp, I was coaxed to go out with a group of campers on a Hobie Cat, and it flipped in high wind. I recall vividly a feeling of total dread as we bobbed in the deep blue and the counselor worked to right the seemingly minuscule, flimsy vessel. I was not a strong swimmer, and, even though I had a life jacket on, the waves were overwhelming. I don't even recall what happened. Did we sail back? Were we rescued by a motorboat? I know I cried. I sobbed, blubbering my tiny tears into indifferent cresting swells. I swore I'd never go out on a sailboat again. (Maybe I did *once*, on a tranquil day ten years later or so, on a Sunfish, with an expert sailor fellow-camper; I have a vague memory of being leery even then.)

I did learn to canoe, and this felt better—more stable, less audacious when it came to speed and distance from shore. Paddling parallel to the shore on flat water seemed respectful of the big lake. I learned to switch places bow and stern, balancing on the gunwales; how to reflip a capsized canoe in deep water using the air trapped beneath the hull, lifting the gunwales straight up while simultaneously swiftly kicking hard in the water and hurling the craft over, ideally empty of all water. When done right, this was a thing to see.

So I grew up canoeing the big lake, and also the inland lakes and rivers each summer, but never really thinking about it as anything very romantic. Heavy plastic green canoes, occasionally a red one, or lighter-weight but clumsier (because longer) aluminum ones, banging on the ground at the put-in, screeching past low-hanging branches while floating down sluggish brown rivers. Ramshackle week-long trips with tasteless Sysco foodstuffs cooked at night over smoky fires. Leeches horrifyingly elastic and bloated, stuck to legs and between toes; leaky dry-bags; soggy sleeping bags; the dank smell of tents encrusted with blood splatters from communally feasting mosquitoes slapped onto the tentwalls season after season, overlapping sepia stains.

Later I was wooed by sea kayaks: they seemed more elegant and sporty. (The colors, alone!) But I never could master the full roll, with that magical twist of the hips. During my early twenties I led kayaking tours in Wyoming, on Yellowstone Lake and on Jackson Lake. These were fairly low-key trips, even if the landscapes were dramatic. Mostly day trips, we would paddle large groups of tourists around interpreting the geography, flora, and fauna—acting like we knew a lot more than we actually did, most of the time. I tried river kayaking once, with a highly skilled friend who had a couple short whitewater boats; after attempting a few moves in the swift current I got slammed into a canyon wall, flipped, and ended up swimming the next few miles.

In Wyoming another part of that job was leading river trips, on inflatable rafts. Our company took a scenic trip down ten miles of the Upper Snake River, on a large raft with an oar rig—this was a meandering journey through meadows and steadily rising foothills just north of Jackson Lake. Then there was a quick three-mile section above that, through a whitewater canyon with some standing waves that peaked in late May and could reach astonishing intensity for a few days (the site of my botched kayaking adventure). I found I was quite good at navigating the smaller inflatable rafts, where we all used paddles (and the guide in the back with a longer paddle commanded the paddlers up-front, aka our "guests" or "customers"). I quickly realized that all those years in crappy canoes with lousy partners in the bow had given me an intuitive sense of how to wrangle a large vessel from a single point of contact with the water. A single paddle blade moved just right can do amazing things.

In the spring of 2013 my father-in-law died, leaving me to more or less tacitly inherit a fifty-year-old Grumman canoe. This was an aluminum, assembly-line-produced piece of art that had been in his family for decades, moving around all along the east coast before ending up here in northern Michigan. The rivets are all still sound, and the keel tracks like it's brand new. Its metal could have become part of an airplane, had more wartime demanded it.

That year I took the canoe out several times on the big lake—on exceptionally calm days, staying near shore. At the end of the summer I took my father-in-law's ashes out on Lake Michigan and spread them where he used to love to swim; the gray ashen mist itself swam and swirled as it descended through fifteen feet of water and disappeared.

The following summer I installed crossbars on the roof our small Subaru, and I started taking the canoe to all the inland lakes I fished every day when I was growing up. I know these lakes like the back of my hand and it was thrilling and delightfully strange to take Julien to these lakes and tell him stories that I dredged up from twenty-some years ago, sense impressions unleashed by sudden flights of sandhill cranes, fish explosions on the lake's surface, familiar cloud formations that tumbled over the forested hillsides.

These lakes lure me back each summer. They are depthless glacial pockets along the lakeshore that beckon to me, not ever with the same message or effect. Part of the Anthropocene is realizing the inescapability of being on the water, in varying senses of that term. This means coastal erosion and melting icecaps as much as dying reefs and rogue tempests. It's how humans are comprised of and depend on water, to a limit. How we maintain awareness of this fact and consciously interact with water—or ignore it, or repress this reality—may be one of the crucial indicators of how the Anthropocene plays out.

Writing about Place

Every spring I get excited and inspired to write about Michigan, when I leave New Orleans and head north for the summer.

Then I get up here and I am almost instantaneously overwhelmed by the borderless expanses of the place. I'm not referring to its geography, so much. I mean it's bigger than Walden Pond, but it's no Yellowstone or Yosemite. I've walked a fair portion of its shorelines (at least on the west side of the peninsula) and have meandered through its various woods and meadows, during all hours of the day and at night. And anyway, people have written good books about entire National Parks and other such privileged or delimited zones before. That's not the problem.

There's something about the saturated quality of this place, all the personal psychological inroads as well as two-track off-roads, the cultural hotspots and weird spaces beyond the grid. I have thought of this book as a twenty-first-century *Walden*, or perhaps better an anti-*Walden*. "Anti-" in the dialectical sense, trying to locate some of the contradictions and tensions within the thinking that Thoreau so well tied to a specific place and its natural registers. But so far, I keep running into nearly impenetrable thickets of things, thoughts, and otherwise thorny obstacles. I suppose it is a good thing—there is a lot I want to write about here, even as it pushes back on me.

For instance, I can't shake that experience of getting lost. It has stayed with me, a mirage memory of being disoriented in the Anthropocene: occasional jet roars far above, traces of human impact appearing and disappearing, and no clear way back to where I came from.

On the map the area doesn't seem so big; the National Park Service barely (and even then, ambiguously) identifies it as part of the national lakeshore, and there are no signs to demarcate the space once you're back there. In person, its valleys and ridges are overwhelmingly enormous. There are not really any trails to speak of, except for meandering deer paths and occasional random four-wheeler tracks that abruptly end, leaving you facing an uncertain infinity of choices in terms of which direction to go. What appear at first to be straightforward slopes turn into Mobius-like undulations that loop back on themselves, and it is just the most uncanny feeling to be unsure of whether you've seen a certain fallen aspen before or if this is a *slightly* different one—and if so, where are you now, it looked like the same place, but you've been walking for ten minutes and you should be somewhere else, unless you got turned around somehow, oh wait, there's a trail ahead, oh no, it's just a slight depression caused by natural drainage after the last thunderstorm ….

These perceptions were especially fresh in my mind when I went back out to this place more recently. While I had never quite shaken off the thrill of being lost (a thrill, of course, because I found my way back), there was another part of those woods that stayed with me: in one of those kettle ponds, when I crept up to the edge of the gin-clear water, I stared wide-eyed as two big (at least for this northern climate) largemouth bass swam within feet of me, looking up at me as if in sheer curiosity. The vision of those fish stayed with me.

So I braved the eerie forest and returned to the kettle pond with my fly rod, only sort of getting lost (but feeling ready to be completely lost again at any moment) along the way. I discovered the pond to be full of bass as well as hybrid (green?) sunfish with larger-than-normal mouths. The fishing was exciting, but it was no walk in the park (even if it was, in a way). First there was the hike there, which was riddled with aporias—at one point I found myself convinced I'd lost my way, and I felt ridiculous standing in a valley of ferns with no water in sight, dumbly wearing my fishing vest and holding my fly rod. But finally, the cedar thicket materialized and the pond was there.

The fishing proper was exhausting and maddening, as the pond is basically a bog mostly surrounded by dense trees; there is no sandy bank to stroll along or wade into. While it appears shallow, the bottom is essentially depthless. You sink right in up to your waist and are surrounded by the tall bulrushes that encircle the pond, whose barbed spikelets manage to routinely grab your fly line, your fly, your shirt … in short, you find yourself totally tangled up about every three minutes.

The bass would shoot across the shallows dramatically and grab my fly off the surface of the water, but then they'd burrow down into aquatic micro-forests of muskgrass, creating the impression of suddenly having the entire world attached to the end of the line. Or they'd take long leaping runs across the pond, reel screaming against my palm. And every time I'd want to move along the shoreline, I had to heave with great effort to break the suction around my feet and legs as I would have slowly sunk deeper into the silt muck as I'd be fishing. And while the fish are relatively gregarious, it's still very easy to spook them; in the glassy water they are used to having to flee from herons, kingfishers, and eagles who perch on branches above the surface.

I'm trying to write this in a way that it isn't merely a fishing story, and isn't simply stock nature writing. I'm trying to both celebrate this place and explode "place" as a concept, as the Anthropocene requires. In the words of Donna Haraway, "What used to be called nature has erupted into human affairs, and vice versa, in such a way and with such permanence as to change fundamentally means and prospects for going on, including going on at all" (40). In Michigan I'm increasingly home sick with this sense of fleetingness, as I reconnect with this place while simultaneously realizing the Anthropocene. I revisit this remote pond on the page, in my mind, knowing all too well that it is a non-simple place, not at all exempt from the pressures that are reshaping the planet. The Anthropocene makes it impossible to write about place.

I was chatting with my friend Ian one day and he mentioned in passing, "writing is impossible." We had been talking about how hard it really is to write clear coherent prose. It is. Difficult, I mean. Just try following your thoughts and sensations for five minutes and putting them into neat prose. Then you add a topic, or god forbid a theme or an argument, and it gets harder still. Focus, attention, word by word, sentence to paragraph. Logical propositions. What was I talking about again?

It's impossible to write about place. I've been trying to write about this little corner of Michigan. Part nature writing, part memoir, part environmental theory, I want this writing to be both a testament to this place and to reflect the thorniness of the Anthropocene.

Nevertheless ... it feels increasingly impossible to write about place.

But now that I think about it, maybe this is why I often begin my freshman writing courses with a seemingly simple assignment: Write about your room. Just describe it as best as you can. How long? I don't know, see how much you can notice, what's around. A sentence, a paragraph, a page ... two pages, three, four—how far can you go? It's an exercise in attention to detail and sustained focus on a single, bounded place. But the boundaries quickly become blurry and elastic. I recall one student last fall who ended up lingering on his dorm window and gradually came to the realization that inside and outside were not as clear and distinct as he'd always assumed. He wondered, did the screws that bolted his window closed count as part of his room? The glass? And if so, just the interior side, or the weather-beaten exterior as well? Impossible to decide.

I was having similar conundrums as I played hide and seek with Julien in the valleys during his fourth summer and as I canoed the inland lakes shrouded in mist. What is this place, at the edge of this peninsula but deep in the heart of the Anthropocene? How can one draw a perimeter around this region, in thought? When does the writing begin, from where should it take off? Writing about place can only etch squiggles and aimless designs in the surface of the Anthropocene.

Hemingwrite

Media theorist Alenda Chang once wrote about the narcissism and "surface tensions" of the Anthropocene, suggesting that we might think about this concept as something to interact with rather than just reflect on. By recognizing the Anthropocene not as a mere mirror but as a touch screen, of sorts, we might manipulate it instead of simply staring into it unto death. With this in mind, I want to take us on a detour.

One day in 2014 I noticed some buzz on Twitter around a device in development called the "Hemingwrite." It was described basically as a stripped-down word processing machine, almost a typewriter, but electronic of course and replete with many of the advantages that we have come to expect from the age of digital media: cloud-based storage, extended battery life, high-resolution display, and so on. As the company explained it on their website,

> The Hemingwrite is a single purpose, distraction-free writing composition device. It combines the simplicity of a 90s era word processor with the modern tech we all require like cloud backups and integration into our favorite document editors like Google docs and Evernote.

The intent of the device was to create an utterly focused *space* for writing: no distractions. No e-mail, no internet, no Twitter notifications, no Facebook pokes, no photo album to endlessly scroll through. Just you and your thoughts—or rather, just your thoughts and a place to put them, as if far from the digital horror of the Anthropocene, where everyone's e-mail in-boxes are full and the bad news streams and overflows. Even if the idea of eluding the Anthropocene was not mentioned explicitly in the ad copy, it was lurking in the background of the tagline for the device: "Set your thoughts free." Free from what? This can only mean free from the crushing reality of modern, networked life that humans have gorged on. (The machine was eventually called the "Freewrite"—and Ian Bogost wrote a brilliant essay about it. But for the purposes of this book, I am lingering on its earlier projected name. For the Hemingwrite ends up telling a Michigan story, one that is a part of my own.)

As I read about the Hemingwrite I wondered why anyone would need this machine, which, let's be honest, would be destined to become simply *another* machine one would have to charge, store, schlep, if to ultimately (hopefully) work on? The Anthropocene, also sometimes called the *capitalocene*, is all about *work*. It seemed to me that it was just another device that the user would end up working *for* rather than *on*.

But as the company frankly puts it, the reason we need this additional device is "Because writing is hard, really hard!" And this is true, as most students, scholars, journalists, and writers will admit: writing is hard, really hard. It takes patience, discipline, and usually some alchemic combination of sleep deprivation, looming deadlines, caffeine (sometimes alcohol), grant funding, free time, quiet space ... and an intangible quotient of inspiration.

The assumption here, in the utopian retrospect implied by the name Hemingwrite, is that writing was *easier* when we had less.

Hemingway becomes a familiar, solitary figure of authorial genius, holed up in a room—*just writing*. Yet the image of Hemingway as a purely focused writer is a myth, a romantic notion of the solitary author genius that we should know is more vexed than it appears, no matter the media moment in history.

Hemingway may not have had Twitter or Instagram, but he was certainly distracted by any number of other things: brook trout, boxing, bulls, beers, barracuda, bicycles, bombshells and so on. We know that Hemingway was a lot more than *simply* a rigorous writer; and, indeed, many of his distractions worked their way back *into* his writings. So how is the imaginary figure of Hemingway as a cutoff, disciplined writer woven into the marketing campaign for this pricey new media object, the Hemingwrite?

On our circuitous route to answering this, another literary clue appears in the description of the device's impressive battery power: It will last for six-plus weeks! We are told that we can "Pull a Thoreau and take the Hemingwrite to your off the grid cabin in the woods." Now things get really confused. We not only need the limitation of no internet, but the device unsubtly urges us *further* off the grid—into the forest, far away. And not simply a century in the past, with Hemingway, but *another* 75 years back in time, in a quieter place, in a rustic, mythic cabin in the woods. *Here*, with the Hemingwrite, with Henry David Thoreau (but also, alone?), we may finally be able to write.

One doesn't need to know too much about Thoreau to have learned that the depiction of him as isolated is, shall we say, an incomplete picture. Thanks to Thoreau scholarship, we know the stories of Thoreau going to eat Mrs. Emerson's pies; we know that what he was working on while he was at Walden Pond wasn't even the book of that name (that came later), but was in fact a book of mourning for his tragically deceased brother, which came to be called *A Week on the*

Concord and Merrimack Rivers. Beyond all this, even if we accept the innocent notion of "pulling a Thoreau" as mirroring whatever finally takes place in the book *Walden*—what is that book actually about?

Walden is essentially a logbook of distractions, a record of the wandering mind and things intruding on any sense of isolation. Thoreau composed a documentary of the collisions and collusions of nature and culture: from the intrusive whistle of the nearby train, to the strange and ordinary "visitors" who pass by; from Thoreau's planted bean rows, to the pickerel in the pond that might be caught (or not). Even though the premise of *Walden* can appear to be writing in seclusion, an observant reader will quickly see that this is a contaminated conceit from the outset. And Thoreau seems well aware of this throughout the book, ironizing his project even as he goes about it. Without saying it anywhere, Thoreau knows the Anthropocene is already well upon us, and he is merely taking notes on its sickening unfolding.

Back to the Hemingwrite out there in a past moment of the internet, a not-so-shiny "retro-modern" new media device that promises to better your writing by cutting you off. As news of the Hemingwrite was circulating, viral tech news for a day, Ian half-quipped on Twitter that *Hemingway* might not be the exact writerly figure the company should attach itself to; he suggested that the device should really be called the DeLillograph. He only had 140 characters (in those comparatively quieter days) to make the remark, so there wasn't any further explanation—but by this I think he meant that the device is really more reflective of the contemporary mediatic concerns of a writer like Don DeLillo than Ernest Hemingway (not to mention Henry David Thoreau).

It is DeLillo, after all, who meditated so shrewdly on the postmodern ambient problems of *white noise*—the electronic, medial buzz that envelops us at all hours of the day, seeping through our machines, creeping into our minds. It is DeLillo who understands the present difficulties of removing oneself from the world picture by any means, as if a *point omega* could ever be located or arrived at. It is DeLillo who imagines how seemingly simulacral data streams can materialize instantaneously, and come crashing into us. It is DeLillo who has written most chillingly about the Anthropocene, fully from *within* the Anthropocene. Needless to say, there was no response to Ian's suggested product name change, and life online went, well, on.

The reason I seized on the Hemingwrite is that it—or rather, its social media marketing campaign in this blip of a moment—happened to evoke two of the rhetorical moves that I had been playing with as I was working on my Michigan book, which then I was calling *Up in Michigan*. The working title was ripped off from a Hemingway short story: a dark and chilling rape narrative that takes place not too far from my home. It's the story that notoriously endeared Gertrude Stein to Hemingway when she first read it, in Paris. Hemingway's Michigan stories accumulated over time, and they are hardly romantic nature stories. In addition to Modernist formal experimentation, they usually involve violent racism, domestic abuse, and cross-cultural tensions. They are little ledgers of the Anthropocene in war-torn landscapes at the edge of modernity.

Still, and awkwardly so, Hemingway is celebrated as a "local" writer throughout northern Michigan. Reading and rereading these stories and teaching them from time to time, I often wonder what we are celebrating when we celebrate Hemingway's ideation of being "up in Michigan." But to get back to our main topic here: Hemingway wasn't writing these stories in a cabin in the woods. Rather, he wrote the bulk of these stories while in France. No distractions there—no, none at all.

At some point when thinking about this, it struck me that the Hemingwrite was poised at the old Derridean juncture of Levi-Strauss's *engineer* versus the *bricoleur*. The Hemingwrite assumes the possibility of the *engineer* as a creator of language and words "out of whole cloth"—an idea that Derrida reminds us is a theological idea, a myth of totality and a secure origin. As if *the book* is ever something that simply springs forth, given the right medium. You have what you need in your head—you don't need anything else. Except this simple device—a place to begin. This *as-if* simple machine that we have stumbled upon, on Twitter. Like, Retweet.

Yet what we see in this most preliminary assessment of the Hemingwrite's marketing campaign is *bricolage* all the way down: All of these myths are cobbled together, each source text, to quote Derrida, "a heritage which is more or less coherent or ruined … ."

In the figure of Hemingway I stumble upon the cluster and clutter of ontological *freeplay*, an entanglement of things and associations in this place. It's the non-basic *structurelessness* of the Sleeping Bear Dunes National Lakeshore. Because there *is* no real border or boundary to this region. It is not about focusing the place or stabilizing it in some secure way, but recognizing and affirming place as, in Derrida's words, an "interpretation of interpretation" and which can never be totalized at a given scale. Can we relate to it in ways better or worse? Yes. Can we fix it once and for all? Absolutely not.

And this means that the Hemingwrite, or any given instrument, will not automatically help one grasp this place, at least not in any determinate form or fashion. Writing place in the Anthropocene means being open to the inescapable difficulties and the necessity of bricolage. It means running into geologic profundity one moment in the guise of a beach stone, or the hard-to-find verdant moose maple—and then it means encountering an eerie deer blind the next moment, a leaning structure that looks wrested right from a Cormac McCarthy novel. It is the archeology of the Hamm Beer can I found floating eerily among lily pads one evening in my favorite remote lake (apparently the can was from the 1950s). And it's the outhouse by that lake's boat launch that was bombed off the face of the planet, possibly by disgruntled Michigan militiamen, or maybe by some devious teenager—no one knows for sure. It's the elusive and delicious morel mushrooms I collect in the month of May, and it's the Lear Jet that screams over my head as it comes to land at the nearby resort airfield. It's my computer glowing at 2 AM while I write, Australian academics chatting with me over Twitter, and whip-poor-will calling off in the woods, threatening to awaken my slumbering children. It's the thunder booming over the bay, and my tracking a storm by satellite radar imaging.

And then, it became the Hemingwrite, too. And then so many more objects, events, and artifacts, accumulating over the years. It's all these things, and they somehow make and unmake a place where I write, up in Michigan. The Anthropocene crisscrosses at all scales, gets tangled up in seemingly simple or pure experiences. It's like a wad of gum that you can't get off your shoes. But it's also your shoes, too. Not to mention your feet. As Bruno Latour sums up the dilemma of the Anthropocene: "There is no cure for the condition of belonging to the world" (13).

My difficulties of writing place became something of a red herring. Or, the difficulties became part of the project, part of the place. A place has to account for all the spurs, all the sudden intrusions and blurry boundaries. Or rather, a place doesn't have to account for these things—the *book* does, to be a coherent thing. This is an admittedly odd task, to go about writing a book about a specific place that the author readily accepts could be resituated ambiguously to *anywhere*. The place falls away from the center. Yet once place is accepted as an uncentered, centerless structure—and if we are determined to not be nostalgic for its origin or for a stable history per se—what can a book about place do, how might it take shape? To rephrase Derrida, the book must surrender itself to the seminal adventure of the *place*—precisely and openly, as place recedes in the overwhelming consciousness of the Anthropocene.

Petoskey Stones

Hemingway being somewhat unavoidable in this place, let's put him to work a bit more. Shortly into Ernest Hemingway's "Ten Indians," one of the Nick Adams stories, we read the following paragraph:

> They drove along. The road turned off from the main highway and went up into the hills. It was hard pulling for the horses and the boys got down and walked. The road was sandy. Nick looked back from the top of the hill by the schoolhouse. He saw the lights of Petoskey and, off across Little Traverse Bay, the lights of Harbor Springs. They climbed back into the wagon again.

What is this place, "Petoskey," that twinkles in the middle distance of this passage? A town, and also a preferred activity in this region: to rove the shoreline looking for the Michigan state stone, the *Petoskey*.

The Petoskey is an aesthetically pleasing, hexagonal fossilized coral from around 350 million years ago. When the stones are dry, the fossil is nearly imperceptible, but when wet the pattern sticks out brilliantly. As I write this I pause to sift through a bunch that I keep on my desk, reminders of Michigan. As Lauret Savoy writes of shale fossils in *Trace*, "The journeys that once-living organisms embark on toward the fossil record, few rarely complete. Happy accidents brought these remains within my reach" (185). So, too, do I contemplate deep time and long journeys as I behold Petoskey stones I have collected over the years.

Wading knee-deep in the clear water along the lakeshore, you can see these unique stones, fragments of a long gone vast coral reef, mixed in with the various and innumerable other rocks that were ground smooth by the glaciers that made the Great Lakes.

Discovering Petoskeys on the beach is fun and stimulating; I can spend hours wandering the shore looking for them and finding them in all different shapes and sizes, usually hurling them back out into the surf as I go. Sometimes I keep one or two particularly striking or unusual ones—my son Julien and my daughter Camille collect them over the summer, and a few inevitably make it back to New Orleans in August. Geologic activity happens in funny ways in the Anthropocene, with little rock chunks flying across continents in Boeings and Airbuses, whizzing down highways in Subarus and Chryslers.

One summer I started finding Petoskey stones in the woods, too. There's something jarring about seeing these ancient fossils lodged around massive tree roots, a mile or two away from the lake. While these rocks are known for being easiest to find along the shore in lapping wavelets, they're really *everywhere* up here, once you start looking. They are disturbing reminders of the vast ice sheets that once carved out this landscape, and which will likely return again at some point in the future.

The Wikipedia entry for Petoskeys mentions that the stones are often made into "decorative objects." Indeed, in shops and farmers market stands around the area you can get all sorts of baubles and trinkets carved from Petoskey stones: bears, butterflies, turtles, fishhooks, crosses, wine bottle stoppers, ear rings, necklaces, even miniature human skulls.

Beyond their use as "decorative objects," though, I wonder if these rocks might also be thought of as *hyperobjects*.

Timothy Morton coined the term "hyperobjects" to describe things that are "massively distributed in time and space in ways that baffle humans and make interacting with them fascinating, disturbing, problematic and wondrous." That's a particularly elegant formulation that applies to so many things that one stumbles across while searching for the Anthropocene. In Michigan, you can hold hyperobjects between your fingers.

Remember, Petoskeys are the remains of a coral that lived around 350 *million* years ago. Let the weight of that time sink into your mind. These beached and subterranean stones that you can see and hold are traces of an aquatic, unfathomable life-form that existed so long ago, in a world inseparable yet totally dislocated from this place that I recognize as home. Pondering this makes my head spin. (To get through the Anthropocene, we may need more head spinning—and more *sharing* of how our heads spin.)

Near the end of Morton's book *The Ecological Thought*, he describes hyperobjects this way: they "do not rot in our lifetimes. ... hyperobjects outlast us all. ... Hyperobjects invoke a terror beyond the sublime, cutting deeper than conventional religious fear" (130–1).

We can use the term "hyperobjects" to describe things like pollution and climate change, things that are terrifying because they seem at once out of our control and longer lasting than us, yet intimately caused by and connected to us, too. But hyperobjects can also be things like Petoskey stones, which by being merely apparent fossils can remind us of vast expanses of time and can spur us to think about how we shape *our own* fossilization.

Morton also says about hyperobjects that "suddenly we find ourselves surrounded by them." I feel this often, with Petoskey stones. Even when I'm holding one of these rocks, I get the strange sense that, really, I'm engulfed by something so much larger than me—and yet, bizarrely, it's in my hands, too.

Here's the thing about the Anthropocene: It's an era that we've named after ourselves. Yet we've named every "era" before it, as well, so in a sense we've named *every* era after ourselves, our situated grasp of things in space–time. It's an act of hubris to name an entire geologic era after ourselves, yes. But perhaps it's also an important turn in that it is an awareness and a *critique* of the naming machine: we name ourselves as the namers, and in so doing, we break a cycle. We stop differentiating ourselves from the planet, the substrate, and start recognizing what it is that we *do* here.

It may seem preposterous to claim planetary prominence, from a way zoomed-out perspective, as if we can *know* just exactly **how** significant we *are*. But from up close—from the microplastics in the oceans to the trash on the beach, from the raked agricultural grids to sweeping networks of energy production, power exertion, and exhaust—it is of critical importance to pause and consider how our species has swept over this planet, leaving only slivers and sometimes vast expanses here and there that feel (but still are not) untouched. The dunes here, the forests, the meadows: they are all enmeshed with the ick of us.

Back There!

The summer when Julien was 2 years old, he learned to forage. First he found the wild asparagus, and he went crazy discovering and devouring the thinnest shoots that punched up through the sandy soil, sometimes barely bigger than his own tiny thumb. The asparagus is back in the valley behind my parents' home, and so Julien learned that the phrase "Back there!" was useful when he wanted to go find more asparagus to munch on.

A few weeks later, the wild raspberries started to get ripe, and "Back there!" took on a new meaning: it indicated a patch of berry bushes in *front* of the house. Then my parents introduced Julien to the herb garden up the hill, and next thing we knew he was naming (and eating) tarragon, parsley, basil, chives, oregano, and dill, all of which were located in an ambiguous, capacious "Back there!"

Arugula and radishes came next, pulled from my father's vegetable garden, to which Julien said "Spicy!" as he reached for more.

Blackberries justly earned their designation of "Back there!" as Julien learned to negotiate the prickly tangle of brambles with his small-body shimmies and twists, all the while grabbing the plump dark berries. His little legs became covered with cuts, which I'm pretty sure would have driven our pediatrician back in New Orleans nuts. But I liked to think of these scratches as spontaneous, random acupuncture treatments—a kind of indeterminate and nonhuman reflexology.

Walking back from the beach one day we passed through the old cherry orchard, tart cherries ripe and hanging within Julien's reach as he perched on my shoulders. I asked, "Julien, did you like that cherry?" He replied, "Mm, mm, *back there!*" Another day my brother-in-law handed Julien a sprig of lavender, and Julien chomped on it—albeit with a quizzical look on his face as the aromatic oil was released. Almost as if a new realm of the back there had been unlocked.

When my younger sister Zane graduated from high school in 2000, a friend gave her a small apple mint plant, and Zane or my mom stuck it somewhere in our yard. Now the apple mints are profuse and constantly spreading—and they are tasty, too, which leads to Julien turning in circles, plucking their lanceolate leaves, pointing and saying "Back there!" to everywhere.

I feel extremely lucky to have this place to return to each summer, where the foraging possibilities are nearly endless. Mid-May is my favorite time of the year in Michigan, when the ephemeral morel mushrooms start to pop and the wild leeks are in full effect. And as Julien has grown up, he has trained his little sister Camille in the art of foraging: on the move, finding scrumptious objects growing all over, sometimes homing in on less tasty things. I'll see them on the hill deshelling errant acorns that then get forcibly spat out; or off in the garden pulling up some particularly spicy radishes that make their eyebrows turn red, and they'll start running in circles hollering for water.

The lessons of foraging add up over time, and they amount to a practical philosophy of place. How to slow down and dig in.

First, how things are limited: once you've eaten all the ripe raspberries, you have to wait until tomorrow for more. So foraging also teaches that there are daily cycles. And when a crop is finally done for the season—when the last chanterelles poke through the leafy forest floor, for instance—we learn about a longer temporal end of things; they'll be back next year. And Julien and Camille are also learning not to trample on things—so that they'll stick around longer *this* year. How to walk delicately over the ground.

Then there is the lesson of how different plants grow in different places. Foraging requires attention to detail—from the foliage and fellow scavenging slugs and bugs, to the shades of colors of leaves and fruits, to the feel of the ground underfoot, the subtle distinctions between sandy and loamy soil. And finally there is the lesson of pacing yourself, so that you don't moan "*belly* ..."—and instead can keep saying "Back there!"

Julien and Camille are learning proximity and distance, where the various bushes and plants are in relation to one another. And they're learning, ever so slowly, to distinguish between ripe and unripe berries, between edible leaves and all too bitter ones. They're learning to forage.

But I'm not so sure how these lessons translate to the Anthropocene, to the full knowledge that most places have become *toxic* places, thanks to our own efforts. In Michigan, ticks are proliferating due to climate change, and pesticides from decades ago, near the cherry orchard, have made certain morel spots more dubious.

I'm leery of Julien and Camille foraging in our backyard in New Orleans, where under the surface of fecund-looking clovers, sour flowers, and nasturtiums lie amalgams of asphalt shingles, wires in knots, wrought iron rusting clusters, ceramic fragments, brick caked in lead paint … all of this jam-packed into what passes as soil, the layer of earth under our home. Back there is nowhere, here. It's all under us, and everywhere.

Dinner Dinner Dinner

Acknowledging the Anthropocene is an admission of complicity, an awareness of being found guilty. Like a planetary game of tag, we are it. And there's no one else to tap, to get out of it.

Back up in Michigan for the winter holidays one year, high winds knocked out the electricity for a couple days. A family friend offered her Blue Apron meals to my parents, since she was out of town. I'd never heard of it: Blue Apron is a gourmet dinner subscription service that sources local ingredients, then packs and delivers the dry-ice-cooled meals, ready to prepare and cook. All you have to do is follow the directions.

My parents prepared the meal at a nearby cottage that still had power and brought the food over in pots and pans. Next thing I knew, we were wolfing down decadent platters of tail-cut salmon fillets topped with dollops of a spritely horseradish sauce. There were garlic mashed potatoes and grilled Brussels sprouts. I opened a Bordeaux, and we supped by candlelight. The power would not come on for several more hours. It was Christmas.

Over the next two weeks, we tried two more Blue Apron meals: a chicken dish (the details escape me) and orange-glazed meatballs with brown rice and bok choy. My mother, who is a plenty good cook on her own, followed the instructions—opening little plastic cups and curiously sized baggies of accessories, and pouring them into mixing bowls and pans in the specified order. The whole experience was shameful; we all turned our eyes downward as the modular meals came together. There was something slightly embarrassing about snapping together these prearranged, picture-perfect meals. Not that everyone who uses these services is doing it for the aesthetics—time saving is a very real ramification of hyper-capitalism when every second can be squeezed for labor and profit elsewhere. And any modicum of time to be saved becomes an entirely reasonable goal in this hellacious cycle of endless work and extraction.

And of course, we're also complicit in this fantasy. The nearby town Traverse City has its own iteration of *Edible* magazine. When we visit family in Michigan, we have access to an extensive vegetable garden and get a weekly share through a nearby farm. Homemade basil and parsley pestos adorn our evening tables; my father massages freshly picked kale with olive oil and sea salt, until it melts in the mouth. At home, we frequent the local farmers markets. Living in New Orleans has meant learning the unique ingredients, flavors, and combinations that define the cuisine (and culture) of this city. It has meant introducing Julien and Camille to the tastes and technics of New Orleans eating—crawfish, okra, red beans, and more.

But here's the thing about dinner: it's often a disaster! The children bicker; someone's in a bad mood and they just don't want to talk about it; the petite tender goes a minute too long and gets chewy; a bowl of penne gets thrown onto the floor from a highchair; you can already tell the wine is going to give you a headache. Usually dinner is a mad scramble, and sometimes it's a pure debacle. And then sometimes, it's perfect.

Blue Apron does something funny to dinner: it turns it into a predictably good thing to make and consume. It seems to come out just right, every time. This is profoundly weird, if you think about it: the idea that every meal should be perfect. Perfect dinner after perfect dinner. What life is this? Blue Apron is just a few steps away from Willy Wonka's three-course meal stick of gum—and you may recall how that turned out for Violet Beauregarde. Blue Apron is an indicator of Anthropocene denial. It wants everything to be uniformly prepared; and it wants express delivery, too.

A century prior to the internet, Gertrude Stein liked to repeat words to the point that their meanings both wobbled and became weirdly visceral, things you'd start to feel in your mouth. I am saturating this book with the word *Anthropocene* even as my search continues, even as it may seem circuitous or scattershot. Anthropocene. Anthropocene. Anthropocene. Each time, it comes out different. Each time, it brings something else into the fore.

Blue Apron might be worth trying, especially if it gets you actually cooking and experimenting with new vegetables, herbs, and spices on your own. Blue Apron ads proliferate on the internet, attempting to yoke the idea of dinner to this brand, in the minds of searchers on the web. But we should not be fooled, or lulled into complacency: Dinner isn't perfect—it's not supposed to come out the same every time, dinner dinner dinner. It's a thing, like any other, fraught with difficulties, nuances, spills, and surprises—and it's also riddled with the economics of the late Anthropocene.

Internet-based sales rely on ad placement saturation, the dissemination not just of products but of symbols and signs of ubiquity. Think of the blooming of Amazon Prime vans, those dark blue creepers with the minimal swoop of the brand on their side panels. The adscape of the Anthropocene is a resplendent beast, metastasizing and repeating itself with no end in sight.

The reality of these services is that they are incredibly wasteful, but they are also indices of a socioeconomic predicament that goes far beyond the lived experience of cuisine or deliveries in any one place.

In fact, such services are the very reality of place having been sold off, too.

Status Unknown

In the summer of 2014 admirable researchers were working to determine the fate of Amelia Earhart's final flight. Meanwhile, up in Michigan, I had a local airplane mystery of my own to ponder.

One morning another business jet roared overhead, banking just over the tree line to the south. It made a low pass over the nearby landing strip, then arced up and circled to make another approach. Pilots often do this here, making a preliminary flyover if they have never landed on the short skinny runway before (there is no air traffic control at the airfield).

Around that time Julien and I were on our way to the farmers market in town, so we took a small detour to see if we could spot the plane. Sure enough, the jet was taxiing down the runway as we drove past the field.

The pilot looked out at us blankly as he taxied by. The plane came to a stop and powered down its engines; the pilot let down the door stairs and looked around—waiting for his passengers, presumably. He wore a rumpled white button-down shirt and a standard captain's black cap.

A quick Google search of the tail number N560CL revealed it to be a Cessna Citation 560, built in 2008 and owned by a corporation in Schaumburg, Illinois. Beyond that, I couldn't find out much. I don't know what I was expecting; but the way it cut in over the trees, the anticipatory emptiness of the waiting plane … there was just something weird about it. Flight Aware recorded the registration details of the plane as "Status Unknown."

When I tried to track the plane's flight path, to see where it had come from and maybe where it was bound, I was met with a message that stated: "This aircraft (N560CL) is not available for public tracking per request from the owner/operator." At the same time, I was invited to "upload photo now." I hesitated and considered uploading a picture I'd snapped as it had taxied by. Instead, I turned back to my phone.

A few clicks away, on the site "Planes and Choppers Photos," one contributor had snapped a picture of this plane back in 2010, and beneath it commented: "Couldn't quite make out the artwork on the tail, but it is owned by International Aviation out of Schamburg, [sic] Illinois."

I had noticed the artwork on the tail, myself: there was a yellow pictograph of a tree and some dancing people next to it, and the words "Celebrate Life" beneath. What sort of blandly positive imagery and language was this, on the tail of a private plane whose status was unknown? On this site again I was invited (and tempted) to "upload a picture."

I understood that it was a private plane, and that therefore public information about it was limited, or even decidedly screened. And I realize that websites like "Planes and Choppers Photos" are all about collecting images and information and making these things available. I understood that the jet I saw that morning was probably banal, an ordinary object of contemporary charter air travel, some millionaire's planned vacation or spontaneous trip.

But still I was intrigued, maybe even a little obsessed with this plane. Perhaps it's exactly the ordinariness about the plane that intrigues me. The fact that for the pilot, it's just another day at work, another anonymous passenger or family to ferry to one place or another. It could be anyplace. The fact that the sudden roar of the jet engines as the plane descended was almost immediately swallowed up by the proximate woods, wind gusts, and bird sounds.

The Citation nagged at me and reminded me of the way that Raymond Carver stages his story "Nobody Said Anything" in creepy proximity to a mundane regional airport, with indifferent planes taking off and landing while smaller tragedies play out on the ground. Here is the main character, a boy playing hooky from school to go fishing in Birch Creek, located "below the airport":

> I went up the embankment and climbed under a fence that had a KEEP OUT sign on the post. One of the airport runways started here. I stopped to look at some flowers growing in the cracks in the pavement. You could see where the tires had smacked down on the pavement and left oily skid marks all around the flowers. (10)

It's this kind of intrigue that I was lured by—this aslant sense of something important happening nearby that is also entirely unrelated to me and disparate from my life, maybe even deliberately elided from view. I wanted to know what the seats look and feel like in that plane; how much the pilot makes per hour; the strangest trip the plane has ever taken; close calls it has had; all the accumulation of unremarkable flights, all the minutes and hours of being that have taken place in and around that small fuselage. But these details were all inaccessible to me—status unknown. That's what made it a mystery worth pondering, local at least for an hour or so. It was indicative of an economic structure that seemed beyond my own life, but roared over it, too.

When we drove back home, we looped back up to the airfield; but the plane was gone. Who was it carrying? Where did it go? I wouldn't get to know. Searching for the Anthropocene is like investigating a mysterious airplane: it's a sense of something having gone *wrong*, even when it all appears to be going exactly as planned.

Meals Ready to Eat

Over dinner one night in New York while visiting my publisher, the topic of hot sauces came up. A well-trod debate ensued concerning the relative merits of Cholula, Tabasco, Crystal, Louisiana, and other more obscure hot sauces. I mentioned that each military issue Meals Ready to Eat (MRE) packet came with a tiny glass bottle of Tabasco—I remembered this from my brief stint working on a National Forest Service fire crew in Wyoming in the summer of 2000. Around the swank dinner table in New York, we speculated as to what sort of deal Tabasco must have cut with the government, and when, to arrange this extraordinary coup.

The next morning at my hotel breakfast buffet, I was astonished to see a small bowl of these very same tiny 1/8-ounce Tabasco bottles. I hadn't seen these things or even thought about them in over fifteen years, and I had vaguely wondered if I'd exaggerated them in my story the night before. But sure enough here they were in front of me. I used one with my breakfast, guiltily leaving most of the contents in the miniscule bottle on the table after I was done. What a waste. Insignificant in isolation, but … I imagined millions of such partially used, incredibly cute glass bottles sparkling in favelas, scarred plains, and rubbish tips around the world.

When I moved to New Orleans, my students at Loyola were still telling stories of eating endless MREs after Hurricane Katrina. There were popular flavors, like Mexican Style Chicken Stew and Asian Beef Strips, and the ones that everyone agreed were disgusting—like Sloppy Joe. My students were simultaneously grossed out and fascinated by the things.

Five years before Katrina, while clearing trails in the Wyoming mountains, I had had my own experiences eating too many MREs: the storehouse had loads of them and we would schlep them up into the mountains with us and devour them after clearing trail for ten hours straight.

Back home in Michigan after my New York trip, and now curious to revisit MREs, I decided to see if I could buy one online. I went to Amazon and searched. There they were, a grid of choices. By the boxful, individual in assorted flavors, mega cases of 24 for $240 … . I ordered a single MRE and waited the obligatory two Prime days. Tommy our UPS guy pulled up the dirt road, hopped out of the truck, and handed me my package. Just another delivery for him, but for me the suspense had been building all morning, swinging Julien and Camille in the hammocks while eagerly waiting for the rumble of the delivery truck.

Inside the house, I tore the box open and then carefully cut off the top of the stiff pouch, laying the contents out on the table. Julien and Camille were enraptured by all the inner packages, the strange monotone green-brown of the plastic. The main course for this one was Beef Stew. I squeezed the lumps of beef in the stew pouch. The peanut butter pouch was strangely familiar, with its weird bendy texture. I kept the laxative gum away from the kids, who were eyeballing it hungrily. It had the Department of Defense seal at the top, right below the "Peelable Seal." It said it was "Warfighter Recommended, Warfighter Tested, Warfighter Approved™." It's always wartime in the Anthropocene. The pine trees whistled outside in the breeze, a freighter rumbled by on the lake horizon. A hawk screamed. I felt foolish for this order, implicated many times over in the murk of knee-jerk consumption. I had thought I might find something critical here, but instead it was a bag of nationalistic emptiness—a false promise of survival.

Perhaps the saddest part was the hot sauce: it was no longer the miniature glass bottle of Tabasco, but a flimsy, miniscule packet of Brulliard's pepper sauce—"made with tabasco peppers." I was so let down. Maybe I shouldn't have been nostalgic, as these newer packets are arguably less wasteful than all those glass bottles. But it also evoked a general cheapening, a devaluing of what was already nearly a zero point of life: surviving on packets of mass-produced food made amid creeping landscapes of destruction.

Nonlinear Dynamics

The Anthropocene is always as much of a social provocation as it is a scientific paradigm. It's a call to responsibility, to acceptance, and to taking action—however small an individual action may seem in the vast, collective, species-size dilemma that such a shift also entails. Each interaction, each relationship, opens up possibilities for a new orientation toward the Anthropocene. If we are open to them. Being up in Michigan—being homesick for a place no longer clear and distinct—continues to present such occasions to me, whenever I am there.

A few times each summer we head up the hill behind our house to have dinner with the Lowe family, whose old brown house is near the top of the hill with a stunning view over Good Harbor Bay. Scott Lowe, a retired religious studies professor (and author of the Object Lessons book *Hair*), makes a delicious vegetarian spread—and other dishes appear, brought by neighbors, along with plenty of wine. Sometimes there are new faces, friends and visitors from afar.

In July 2017 a rental car pulled up the drive during the Lowe feast, spruce cones crunching beneath tires. A couple got out of the car and gave Scott and Mary Beth big hugs, and they were henceforth introduced all around. Scott quickly brought the guy over toward me and said, "This is my best friend from college, George Sugihara—he loves fly-fishing! Hey, why don't you take him fishing tomorrow morning before they leave?" It's not hard to convince me to go fishing—but to be honest, I don't really like fishing with too many other people. Greg Keeler; my friend Glen from the food Co-op in Traverse City; my buddies Nathan and Brian in New Orleans. The list runs out fast. But trusting Scott, and feeling a good vibe from George immediately, I agreed and we made plans—I'd be at the top of the hill at 4:45 a.m., and he'd be ready.

A storm blew through overnight, leaving a lingering cool wind and drizzle when I woke up at 4:25 a.m. Not ideal conditions, but I wasn't about to give up a chance to get out to the lake, even though the morning did not bode well for fishing. (The fish tend to be less active after a storm like this.) I wasn't sure if George would still want to go, but we exchanged text messages and he was all for it. I quickly dressed, made two thermoses of tea, jumped in the car, and drove up the hill to the Lowes. George was ready with his bamboo rod and ancient waders; he climbed in the car and we coasted down the hill and drove on into the park.

By the time we waded into the shallows, the rain had let up but the wind was still disturbing the surface of the lake. The water temperature had turned over—so top-water fishing for bass, my favorite technique here, would be ineffective. And we had both brought lightweight rods, so we weren't going to cast big minnow patterns for pike. I was flustered, but luckily George was just happy to be out on the water, getting his cast back in shape and catching occasional small bluegills in still pools near reeds. We got to talking about George's work at Scripps: teaching and researching ecology, especially applying nonlinear dynamics and complexity theory. I told him I was working on a book on environmental aesthetics, and I mentioned that I was studying a bit of landscape ecology. George said something like, "Oh, I wrote one of the early papers that established landscape ecology as a field."

Wading along the shoreline, George described how any holistic understanding of a natural system must account for multiple dynamic attractors. I couldn't follow it all, but as George told me about some of his research findings it all started sounding vaguely like Timothy Morton's more recent work—coming from a very different discipline, but oddly akin. The basic idea for both is that life is not linear and correlation does not mean causation—even when things *appear* to be otherwise. Individual units or beings are in fact complex archives of long-term, dynamic relationships with other entities and variables.

George's "empirical dynamic modeling," where you start with relatively simple observations and data, started to sound weirdly like Tim's recipe for ecological *attuning*, where "a thing is dappled with time" and thus provides opulent material for observation, but also all sorts of gaps and irregularities that likewise make whatever is under observation become weird, fuzzy (*Veer Ecology*, 164). I may be simplifying things too much. I might be reaching for a parallel or connection between the hardest science and the supplest environmental philosophy. But this is how it struck me at the time—and how it strikes me still.

A year and a half after this outing, I got back in touch with George over e-mail and asked him about the Anthropocene. George wrote back that he was adamant about "the need to usher the transition from 20th century deductive science toward a more inductive 21st century science. I see the 20th century presumptive approach, which is the basis of how we think, as arrogant. We need to be more humble …" (personal correspondence). In this I felt a kindred spirit, trying to urge humans away from *all* the patterns of thought and progress of the twentieth century, into something radically different.

That night I had a strange dream. I dreamt I was standing at the end of a dune cliff at the edge of Lake Michigan, steeper than any I'd ever stood on. I was talking to George, and he was explaining his e-mail to me, how "*the normal way we try to understand nature (our conceptual habits) may not apply.*" The sand was eroding under me, and I was struggling to keep balance. The surf crashed below, ready to take me under. And I was ready to let go, to be a sacrifice to the losing gods of the Anthropocene—or food for the fishes, at the very least.

Waste

This past summer there were drones over the lake. One day we hiked down to where the mouth of a favorite creek meanders into Lake

Michigan, and as we approached the beach I first heard it: "*EEEEEE EEEEEEEEEEEEEEEEEEEEEEEEEEEEEEEEEEEE.*" That's the best way I can describe the sound of the quadcopter hovering about 30 feet over the water, a teenage boy holding the remote control and guiding it out a ways and then back toward the shoreline. He was apparently taking a video of his friend on a paddleboard. But it's illegal to fly drones on the national lakeshore, and someone must have told the boys, because a few minutes later they were packing up the machine and tramping off toward the parking lot. Still, the eeriness of the surveilling drone lingered, and I couldn't concentrate on catching crawfish with Julien and Camille. Elsewhere in the world around this time, drones were being flown perilously close to airports, being taken out of the sky by territorial raptors, and ending up in trash heaps as they burn out, crash, break their propellers.

Out in the woods one afternoon, I looked down and I finally found it, or at least I glimpsed it for a moment: the Anthropocene was right here, crystallized in a cheap pocket knife, lost twenty-five years ago and now resting on the ground among the fronds of some bracken ferns. I had been wandering aimlessly on this hillside when I looked down and there it was—dropped long ago, suddenly back in my possession. It's just a crappy old lock-blade pocket knife, probably bought for five or ten dollars from the Totem Shop—but its sheer tenacity, lying there amid the pine needles and fiddleheads, struck me in the gut, shanked me. It reminded me of a question posed by Timothy Morton in *Being Ecological*: "Can you think of anything more uncanny than realizing that you are in a whole new geological period, one marked by humans becoming a geophysical force on a planetary scale?" (5). It was just a small single object, but it was dragging a whole culture of habits and patterns right behind it.

***

On the beach I walk with the Anthropocene. Balloon strings and straws, zebra mussels and dead gobies. In the shallows of my favorite lake I see the Anthropocene: spent shotgun shells in myriad colors. In the meadow I find the Anthropocene: three ragged tires in a line, marking a border or edge of ... something long gone. But the tires remain, white-rimmed and grass growing through the centers. In the red pine woods I find the Anthropocene: eerie rows that appear out of nowhere and which go nowhere, too. Searching for the Anthropocene is really just a matter of living in the Anthropocene, living with a sense of its nagging presence, like becoming attuned to the trash that litters the lakeshore here, washing up anew each morning, impossible to keep up with—unsightly stuff, sometimes bleached to a natural hue, sometimes garish orange and fluorescent blue. Bottle caps, deflated balloon bodies and frayed nylon cord, plastic drinking straws bent in half, Big Gulp cups, strange nozzles and fasteners, fishing lures with mangled treble hooks, bottled water bottles torqued into muscular transparencies, shredded candy bar wrappers, never satisfied, more straws, fragments of car bumpers, potato chip wrappers, Styrofoam, whorls of plastic strips, spent tape cylinders, plastic shotgun shells, mouths agape. None of this is mine, exactly—but neither can I separate myself from these abject things.

Polish writer Olga Tokarczuk refers to this sort of colossal, dispersed waste as nothing short of the origin of a species: "The planet's witnessing the appearance of new creatures now, ones that have already conquered all continents and almost every ecological niche. They travel in packs and are anemophilous, covering large distances without difficulty" (396). Tokarczuk is referring specifically to plastic bags, but she might as well be talking about the dunes of plastic detritus that I find on the beaches of this national lakeshore each morning, unceasing and apparently increasing—or at least amassing, migrating everywhere.

***

My old pocket knife, pressing down inertly on the ground all those years, indicts me in this mess. As do the toy drones that Julien would become enamored with a year later, begging to fly, and which I would not be able to resist.

Perhaps one of the most difficult lessons in searching for the Anthropocene is that there is no clear lesson, no succinct takeaway—other than that we humans have garbled things terribly, and that arresting this trajectory will take immense work and adjustment. And all the waste—we cannot ever simply escape it, dump it elsewhere. Even as we have invented technological marvels and made human life comparably luxurious for a lot of the population, we have risked a future for this same species. Even as we have managed to protect and champion some reserves of wilderness and wildlife, like the Sleeping Bear Dunes, we have decimated countless other places and lifeforms in the process. We cannot keep doing this, but not all that we have done can be so easily abandoned or aborted. And some things we might actually *want* to keep—keep around, keep doing, keep on going.

Into this impossible situation I write, searching for the Anthropocene. I write to try to memorialize and think through a place I love; and I write to expose and critique an activity that has become natural to us, unquestionable: the frantic production of waste. I'm not innocent in relation to either of these realms.

Lone Wolf Theory

During the summer and into the fall of 2016, when I'm out fishing alone, I hear the chattering of semiautomatic rifles, off in the woods. Target practice, showing off. Occasionally there'd even be a burst of full, manic machine gunfire—someone's illegal or heavily modified weapon, practicing for the apocalypse. Auditory reminders of fierce individuals exercising their right to bear arms. It's the specters of self-defense and government coercion that usually motivate these gun owners. Of course, sometimes it's also a love of the intricacy and art of weaponry. Regardless of the philosophical underpinnings, these things are increasingly haunting our lives in the Anthropocene, far beyond rural gun clubs or sandlot shooting zones. And they make their way into ecological concepts, in common expressions—like the phrase "lone wolf."

The shooter was a lone wolf. This expression proliferated after the Las Vegas massacre of 2017. But what *is* a "lone wolf?" The phrase may be used to signify that someone has operated without clear political or ideological motivations. But here's the thing: "lone wolf" as a concept is precisely a political and ideological fantasy. Sometimes we want to be a lone wolf so as to seem extraordinary; and at other times we want to label someone a lone wolf in order to marginalize them. A lone wolf sounds like someone who can dodge the Anthropocene, escape or short-circuit a worst-case scenario.

But the idea of a person existing in isolation, or able to achieve something on their own, holds up the entire "free market" ideology and every political argument that subtends and supports such an economy. The notion of a lone wolf imagines that a person can merely linger in a freely moving state, somehow within and yet beyond all the normal strictures and structures of society. This theory also dismisses the lines that cross over and complicate this free state: capital flows, food and waste networks, gun and ammunition supply routes, firearm modification tools and techniques, communications platforms, and interactive systems.

Taken literally, "lone wolf" is also a curiously *naturalizing* phrase. It turns the person into an animal, a predator—ah, but here we've already admitted the non-aloneness of the lone wolf, as a predator by definition requires *prey*. And an animal requires an ecosystem. The lone wolf postulates cause and an effect, clear and distinct: there is a hungry predator and vulnerable prey. Yet even as this complicates the myth of singularity, the narrative manages to get absorbed into a trope.

To have a lone wolf, we need not only a flourishing ecosystem with a range of species but presumably also a wolf *pack* at least somewhere nearby. An isolated organism simply could not occur, and if this *appears* to be the case we must look for other members of the species as they most certainly exist.

In this case the lone wolf is no aberration at all. The pack is dispersed but evident: individuals who mistake individuality for first priority and who have internalized personal preference as a default modality. But an outward-looking investigation, such as this, is then not useful because it implicates more of them, more of *us*.

Call it the Anthropocene or globalization, or just call it living on a planet: We *know* that things are more enmeshed, more confused, less isolated. Even if we would *prefer* things like "America first," the slogan contains a hidden admission that there is a second, third, fourth, and so on—a list of other entities which it turns out may not be so easy to order and rank. There are always *more* of us around, aiding and abetting, giving and taking. And to rank becomes an act of violence.

The phrasing was tweaked and strengthened, and the lone wolf of the Las Vegas shooting was described to have committed an "act of pure evil." This is an ultimate *othering*, an effort to cast out once and for all. As if such a thing can be decisively identified and routed.

Yet, how would a pure act cross over to the impurely evil realm, namely over to the land of the free? If the act were *purely* evil how did it get entangled with everything else that is assumedly *good*? If something pure can be tainted, was it ever really pure in the first place? All of this, in *Sin City*.

Things are not static. That's part of the problem with the Anthropocene, and it's also a problem with the lone wolf theory, and with the accounts of the events that took place in Las Vegas that terrifying night. The lone wolf theory is a linear model but ecosystems are complex, with shared driving variables. The flourishing ecosystem in which the lone wolf appears to thrive is a culture of gun idolization and fetishization, of viral media and visual technologies, short-term residency and idle pleasures. There is no lone wolf. There are known attractors (mass shootings) and available mechanisms (guns). There are established patterns (confusion, chaos, outrage, mourning) and ready outlets (TV, social media, op-eds). As I write this, I necessarily become part of the matrix. But I already was a part of it, through my seemingly passive consumption and spectation, especially on social media.

The lone wolf is not used to signify a dynamic entity but rather is a rhetorical maneuver that seeks to freeze and contain the subject. But the lone wolf is also an existential costume that one can put on. However, to don this garb is to require its legibility: namely, the gaudy context of recognition, fear, replication, perhaps even warped admiration. For, it is no coincidence that the leader who conjured the expression "act of pure evil" has also been described as a lone wolf.

Later, if inconsistently, the lone wolf was called "sick." This is a contradictory descriptor, though, because the lone wolf is by nature a *healthy* designation. Regardless of whether the lone wolf is imagined to be operating with ill or admirable intents, the figure is a rugged individualist, a naturalist icon of sorts.

Yet to pathologize the lone wolf is to raise questions about symptoms, and this too disturbs the model. Symptoms can turn out to be inseparable from an illness and its environment; where the discrete body begins or ends cannot be easily diagrammed. If "sick" functions as an abject pejorative, it also insinuates the lone wolf *as* a body into a *bigger* body. What is the scale of this sickness?

The lone wolf theory asks for a linear understanding of the world: a predator charges in and wreaks havoc on a community. Or, conversely, a lone wolf takes charge, drains the swamp, and returns things to a previous (imaginary) point of balance and normalcy. Either way, it is imagined as a one-way causal chain—even if unplanned or unanticipated.

But life on our planet doesn't work like this. Even as time seems to march forward and as things may appear to be linear or neatly causal, the trajectories within are always dynamic and manifold. So, recourse to singular members of specific species does not help matters. Metaphors can only get us so far, and not necessarily in the right direction.

Are you a dove or a hawk, an elephant or a donkey? Is the market bearish or bullish? Can a lone wolf also be a red herring? These animacies are neither innocent nor innocuous in their attempts to describe a set of straightforward affairs. Even through innuendo, such caricatures suggest an unconscious acknowledgment of complex ecosystems where real animals coexist in fraught and dynamic form. Humans not excluded.

We must admit and account for the dynamism of the situation—of "situations" in general as matters of scale. The task is difficult but necessary if we are to not fall into traps of linear thinking. The woods are full of such snares, if not of lone wolves.

One marker of the Anthropocene will be how we have dealt with our dead. Future discoverers of cemeteries, mass graves, and missing planes will wonder about our methods and modes of handling the dead. So many grids and uneven splays of bodies will end up fossilized. What will these forms bespeak of our patterns of life—and death? For all our imagination and inventiveness, how might we be seen overwhelmingly as a vicious and violent species?

War Birds

I wake up before dawn, listen for wind in the trees, and when I ascertain that it is still, and Julien, Camille, and Lara are all sleeping deeply, I slip out of bed, dress quietly, open and close the creaky door carefully, and head to one of my favorite lakes. This lake is isolated in the park, no houses or other human structures visible from its shores. At one point it was probably part of Lake Michigan, but was cut off from the big lake by dune succession or some other quirk of glacial erosion.

I go out to this lake to fly-fish, but it isn't the kind of fly-fishing you might have seen in *A River Runs through It* or on a TV sports channel. This isn't the sort of fly-fishing that the *Wall Street Journal* once reported on, in an article called "How the Rich Fish," about custom-made trout streams that run through multimillion dollar properties near premier tourist destinations.

My fly-fishing outings on these shallow glacial waters along the Lake Michigan lakeshore are slower endeavors, less action-packed than the fly-fishing often celebrated in popular culture. I frequently hear people describe fly-fishing as an art, but usually this presumes slow-motion casting against romantic mountainous backdrops, rapid river water sparkling. I fish when the water is dead calm, and the horizons around me are obscured by banks of reeds and rushes, cattails and submerged dogwoods. The casting isn't pretty, even when it needs to be precise: my fly aimed to land in a one-square-foot pool in the midst of dense aquatic vegetation, the fly line draping over exposed stems and water lilies.

On this particular lake, I wade about a half-mile along the shoreline before I reach the spots that I like to fish. These are a series of spillover ponds that are a foot deep at most, and which join the main lake through dense stands of reeds that are mere inches deep. It's a wonder that the fish can get back into these inner pools, but the beavers carve hidden channels leading to their lodges, thereby making the shallow ponds navigable to even the largest bass.

As I move through the water, I see fellow creatures: several deer clomp through the shallows on the opposite shore, watching me quizzically; a pair of sandhill cranes make their way delicately along the line of reeds, twenty feet in front of me and seemingly unconcerned by my presence; a loon jets by overhead, and lands on the far side of the bay; a pair of swans cruise by, their giant wings emitting a low-vibration whine eerily familiar, calling to mind the moan of an Airbus's turbofans on descent. Then there are damselflies and dragonflies that skim the surface of the lake, occasionally dipping into it and leaving a ripple, or sometimes themselves if they don't extricate their wings soon enough from the water—then they become breakfast. Around the lake I hear an occasional slurp as a dragonfly or damsel fly is sucked down from the surface.

It is one of these insects that I am trying to imitate with my fly, lying it down so it skips once and then rests on the surface, appearing to be stuck but still alive, quivering. After letting it be still for about fifteen seconds, I'll give it a little twitch, to signal life. When I do it right, I can often see a dramatic *V* racing toward my fly, a moment of stillness, and then the water opens up and my fly is taken by a bass, or sometimes by a large sunfish. More rarely, a northern pike attacks the fly, broad brown back bulging out of the lake as it slashes, which often slices right through my tippet with its razor-sharp teeth—fortunately leaving the fly bobbing in the wake, and the pike living to see another day. This fishing is methodical and requires stealth and accuracy; it isn't lazy bobber fishing *or* rapid river trout fishing. It is quiet and meditative, and then explosive and intense.

I fish for a while, catching several nice bass and a few plump sunfish, and releasing them back into the warm water. The clouds have faded from sunrise pink to moody, rain-laden gray. And then it happens: I am startled by a tremendous *BOOM*! that echoes over the lake and reverberates off the hillside.

I register this intrusion to the acoustic landscape—the vociferous redwing blackbirds are suddenly silent—and in the same instant I identify and recognize it: I know what this sound is. It is the blast of a hobby cannon that fires 10-gauge blanks, and it is used to wake up the campers at a nearby summer camp. I know this because I was a camper there for many years when I was young, and later a counselor; indeed, I fired that very cannon myself, countless times.

The cannon at this camp is fired at 7:00 a.m. sharp, after which the campers are required to shuffle down to the beach and do exercises followed by a dip in the usually very cold Lake Michigan. Looking back, it seems both quaint and horrifying—the whole routine, but especially the cannon blast. I'm affronted on several levels. There's the sheer noise of it, which interrupts the serenity of the morning. And not just this morning: *every* morning of the summer this blast erupts through the forest and over the hills, sonically disturbing the national park. I wonder about the effects of this percussive sound on all the other lifeforms that inhabit the area.

Then I think about the campers, boys ranging from 7 to 17, who spend three, four, or the full seven weeks there. (There is a girls' camp, too—but the girls are woken up ten minutes before the boys, with a bugle call instead of a cannon.) Considering this mode of waking up, abruptly and by way of a deafening detonation, again and again and again—how can this be good or healthy, especially over time? But then there is another layer to this camp: It is a camp for young Christian Scientists, and so "health" is a strange, mystified, Platonic quality—infinitely reserved within a spiritual realm ruthlessly opposed to the material world. And so my worry about the well-being of the campers' ears and psyches, as affected by the daily cannon blasts, would be easily dismissed and rebuffed by the camp staff. If the cannon elicits an unconscious fear of authority while also building discipline—all the better, from the camp's religious perspective (whether clearly articulated or not).

As I continue to fish, I mull over the aggravating implications of this cannon, and my own imbrication in its existence. Why didn't I argue against this militaristic device when I was a counselor at the camp? I was in college at that time and rapidly shedding the religious beliefs around which I was raised. Surely I should have been able to recognize the strange violence of this cannon, perhaps seemingly innocuous but with ambient consequences. I consider writing a letter to the camp, suggesting that they abandon the practice—out of respect for the aural environment, if for no other reason. But this would be a fool's errand, as the camp remains fiercely tied to many of its traditions even as attendance withers each summer, as church membership wanes, and as long-stay camps like this one go out of vogue, in lieu of sport camps and other vacation activities.

Later that day I am on a walk with my children in the woods behind our home, looking for chanterelle mushrooms. They have just started to appear, and they are tricky to find as they hide beneath carpets of oak leaves. It takes a while to collect a bagful of the smallest chanterelles, but they are worth it—so tender and delicious when they are small, no bigger than the tip of a finger. On our way back, we pause at a dead and decomposing big tooth aspen; Julien has found a stick that he calls a "chop axe" and he starts whacking the downed tree. Camille wants to join in, and so I find her a suitable truncheon and she lays into the log, as well. They are happily chopping away, gleefully turning the tree into compost, when I hear an approaching roar.

At first I assume it is the local millionaire's private jet that lands at the nearby airfield—"Celebrate Life." But then it gets louder and louder, and I remember a split-second before I see it that it's the 4th of July weekend, and Traverse City will be hosting its annual (and increasingly controversial) air show. But it's not a Navy Blue Angel or an Air Force Thunderbird—it's a different model jet, *incredibly* loud and with a straight wing. It thunders by so close overhead that I think for a moment it is about to crash. Right behind it comes another one; it cannot be higher than 500 feet above ground. I look over at my children, and Camille is grimacing. Julien has dropped his chop axe and yells "*What is that?!?*" I'm not sure, but I recognize the shape of some sort of small bomber or machine-gunning plane … the kind of plane they send in to clear out villages on the other side of the world. And yet, now, maybe my own village? Why not? The planes work the same way, the weapons just as effective here as there. They've found me!

When I look it up later at home, my hunch is confirmed: they were A-10 Thunderbolt "Warthogs," a type of warplane designed around a specific rotary machine gun, the 30mm GAU-8 Avenger. It's all there, in the name: these planes were made to get close to the ground and blow up tanks and mow down people. The bullets for the main gun are enormous—each full round well over a foot long and the shells the diameter of a child's arm. They are terrifyingly loud airplanes, and while I had never seen one before in person, somehow I knew immediately what it was—recognized, I'm ashamed to say, from some war movie I saw once.

But in that moment we sit there in the woods, rattled. Our forest idyll has been shattered. It reminds me of some lines in Hemingway's novel *For Whom the Bell Tolls*, when Robert Jordan is watching warplanes fly overhead: "They move like no thing there has ever been. They move like mechanized doom" (87).

Though to be honest, the idyll was shattered earlier that morning, on the lake—with the cannon resounding over the hills. And even earlier, still, in my childhood, specters of war always nearby. In my old childhood toys, the tiny Micro Machine tanks and bombers. The cannon at summer camp. My slingshot from the Totem Shop. My

Hardy Boys book called "Deathgame," with its paramilitary plot. Books about the war in Vietnam. And always, airplanes overhead: military, commercial, private—never entirely certain.

***

There is nothing quite like the sight of the Sleeping Bear Dunes out the window seat, on a flight from Minneapolis to Traverse City, or even better, from the cockpit of a small plane flying along the coast. Yet I also know that this place is mired in farther flung flight paths, the place always leaking beyond its borders, like contrails in the sky spread out to the point that they are indistinguishable with the cloudscape, ever changing itself even as the thunder of jet engines fades away.

Another perspective: this may sound counterintuitive, but it can be hard to see the Anthropocene from the window seat of an airplane at 30,000 feet. Everything, even urban grids and highway systems, seems to flow in and out of the contours of the planet. Irregularities and strange geometries blend into organic patterns. But at the same time, the observing passenger is in a machine that is integrally part of it: creating this as-if sublime view is always also in the service of propelling the Anthropocene ahead. If this epoch ends up being a relatively short one, it will be in part because our planes were so fast and flew so high.

Drawing Lessons

During Julien's eighth summer on the planet, and Camille's fourth, when the two of them would squabble or when they'd moan about being bored, having nothing to do, I'd pack a little lunch, fill up the water bottles, and we'd head out deep into the woods. We'd hike through the valley behind my parents' house, past the wild grape vines and sumac groves, and into the darkness of the maple forests. Up the old logging trail and all the way to the top of the ridge, the second highest point on the peninsula. From this height, through occasional cracks between the dense foliage, we look down at Good Harbor Bay stretching toward the horizon. It's cooler back in the woods, and once we're back here amid the giant beech, northern red oak, and sugar maple trees, life takes on a strange tingling quality. We sit down and eat our sandwiches and apples, and drink water. The longer we are quiet and still, the more new sounds we hear: the hermit thrush, a ruffed grouse whomping over the ridge, a chorus of cicadas, an unidentifiable screech. The breathing and moving of the very trees.

When Julien and Camille start to get antsy, I pull out two drawing pads and pencils, and I take them to different perches, 25 feet or so apart. I tell them to draw what they see, whatever they see, however they want. They immediately jump to the challenge: heads up and down, scribbling madly. I sit on a stump a ways off, reading or just observing.

Here we are, creatures of the Anthropocene, attuning to this world, to the creatures and textures we can perceive in this terrestrial place. I hope my children are learning to appreciate all this, as they sit and draw. The point isn't to perfectly render the scene or capture a landscape or even a still life. It's just to *be* there, aware of the entities and relations that include us and exceed us. My wish is that Julien and Camille will draw from these experiences out in the woods, to grow up to care more for this life, this world—and to recognize their inescapable role in the Anthropocene, if to also consciously wind it down.

The Sleeping Bear Dunes have never been simple, were never isolated from global dramas. My deep love for this place can also be understood as quaint enjoyment, barely cognizant of how the dunes became, at some point along their glacial journey, entangled in the mesh of the Anthropocene. Increasingly I am seeing them this way, wondering about their future. Wondering about my children's future, with this dunescape … and all the world that extends from and is connected to it. How might Julien and Camille relate to not only this place they call their partial home, but by extension other places, even "places" that defy our current understanding of "place" as a discrete thing? In her book *The Mushroom at the End of the World*, Anna Tsing writes: "The concept of the Anthropocene both evokes this bundle of aspirations, which one might call human conceit, and raises the hope that we might muddle beyond it. Can we live inside this regime of the human and still exceed it?" (19). This bundle is what I find when I return home each summer, some winters, all too aware of the rumble and roar of the still persisting vehicles of human progress, machines and operators desperately churning to move the species forward—unknowingly toward a precipitous edge.

Part II
Jet Lag

As much as I love where I'm from, I increasingly can't experience or even think about northern Michigan as a discrete region or serene place, a "home" in any settled sense of the word. Because its boundaries and features have become infected with traces of the Anthropocene. Every encounter is punctured by an explosion of one type or another—and wherever I go, however far into this place I delve, I find the scars and debris of human negligence.

So I turn to another place, or rather what Marc Augé once famously termed a "non-place": the airport and the whole ensemble of experiences and sensations that occur around human flight.

Air travel remains an iconic ultramodern experience, an experience that can also quickly turn into existential vertigo. I've spent a lot of time thinking and writing about airports, and here I find myself back in this realm once more—but juxtaposed with my sickness for home and framed by the nausea of the Anthropocene. I want to track a cumulative feeling of jet lag, at once an intimately personal symptom and widely dispersed cultural phenomenon.

In his book *Anthropocene: A Very Short Introduction*, Erle C. Ellis describes noticing how across widening academic and artistic circles, the "Anthropocene had become a very strange new word indeed" (142). The following pages agitate this strangeness, making the

Anthropocene reverberate against the walls of terminals and within the interiors of new and aging aircraft.

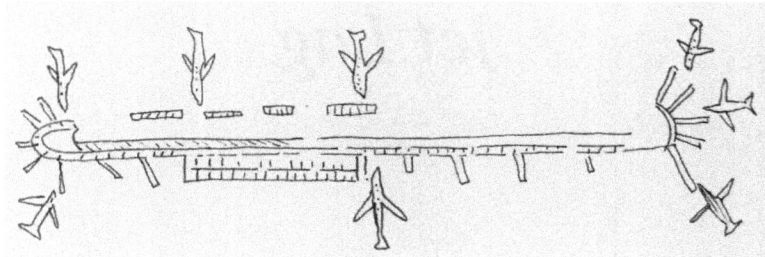

Figure 3 *Even the most generic terminal is key to the Anthropocene. Illustration by Lara Schaberg.*

The Secret Life of Airports

Someone once told me, or maybe I read somewhere, that the runway pattern of the Denver International Airport is visible from space. Regardless if this is strictly true, among all the conspiracy theories that cluster around the Denver airport—Masonic ciphers, neo-Nazi murals, underground missile silos, fallout shelters, and so on—the geographic fact of its vast proportions is something that will last. Long after humans are gone, the stamp of the runways and infrastructure will remain, an awkward ecotone interrupting the plain and abutting the front range of mountains. *That* is the real conspiracy of the Denver airport.

As indices of human impact, airports play a key role in grasping the concept of the Anthropocene. As Olga Tokarczuk writes in her book *Flights*, "They say that you have to sacrifice some living being when you build an airport … to ward off catastrophe" (64). Tokarczuk is onto something here, in speculating about how airfields are always a harsh jolt to their local ecosystems. It's more complicated than this, though. The secret life of airports is less clear than specific catastrophes warded off or happened upon: plane crashes, extreme weather events, hijackings. Instead it has to do with something more unsettling, if also more mundane.

There's a minute-long scene in the 1992 film *Home Alone 2*, starring Macaulay Culkin in his reprise as Kevin McAllister, that sums up the secret life of airports. The scene occurs toward the beginning of the movie, after a frantic race to the airport at which point Kevin's family just barely makes their flight to Florida, bound for a sunny winter holiday. They all make the flight—that is, all except for Kevin. In this scene, Kevin realizes that he ended up on the wrong plane and has landed in the wrong city. Displaced, disoriented, dejected—simultaneously hyper-mobile and out of control. Just another day late in the Anthropocene.

In the opening moment, we see Kevin in the airport seating area realizing he isn't where he should be. The skyscrapers in the background should be palm trees. A split-second later, Kevin leaves, but the seating area remains for a flash: the airport lingers, without our main character and utterly indifferent to the plot of the film. The other lone, waiting passenger in this scene doesn't even register that Kevin has come and gone. It's really a fascinating visual effect—as if the baseline reality of the airport somehow holds together the entire narrative. Of course, in a way it *does*. And not just for *Home Alone 2*: As you may recall, the plot of the original *Home Alone* was *also* driven by an air travel blunder, when Kevin is left home after a faulty headcount as the family loads into the airport shuttle. Both of the original *Home Alone* films are also stories about lacunae opened up by airport logistics. But let's get back to the scene in question.

The next second of the scene changes locations, from the waiting area to the American Airlines customer service desk. What unfolds is a complex montage replete with angry passengers in the background berating an airline employee, and another employee in the foreground multitasking and about to be interrupted by a frantic Kevin. A pot of festive poinsettias in the middle of the frame are almost laughably vivid and cheerful in this cold, sterile setting of ordinary airline transactions. I'm going slow here, but trust me: the Anthropocene is vivid in this scene.

What follows is an awkward exchange whereupon Kevin finds out where he is—and realizes that he is far away from his family. The changing facial expressions of the airline employee suggest a veritable anthology of attitudes, moods, and reactions. What happens over the course of those eighteen seconds or so is itself a primer in the secret life of airports, a complex state of being that conditions and shapes this brief, otherwise throwaway exchange: panic, plea, disdain, resignation—all the stages of Anthropocene awareness, consolidated in a single interaction.

The scene swerves back into the seating area, Kevin having gone back to sit and collect himself. For a moment, the airport seems astonishingly barren and self-evident. Even the other waiting passenger is gone. What do all the empty seats say? They bespeak the rote alienation of airport life, whether experienced over a mere few seconds or sustained for dull minutes or torturous hours. Another feature of the Anthropocene: a glutted globe, yet so much aloneness.

So the scene returns to where we started, more or less. Kevin is again in the waiting room, where he has to contemplate his newly realized fate: he is alone in New York City. Over the next few frames, we see as if into Kevin's head, as he adjusts to a gradual realization: *Wait ... alone, in New York City?!?*

What happens here is a stark reversal in comportment, an effect aided by the neutral environment. Kevin goes from shocked to something like tickled, as he considers the fact that he is alone in New York while his family is far away in Florida. The airport facilitates this reversal in subtle ways. By being so crushingly plain and stark—the uncomfortable seats, the severe internal framing of the plate glass windows—the airport pressurizes the time and space, so as to maximize the force of Kevin's transformation: from totally out of control to completely owning his trajectory. (Another Anthropocene delusion.)

This is a common enough phenomenon in airports, one that most people have probably felt, but often in its obverse form: usually people experience such a transformation when they go from giddy travelers in motion to strung-out, stranded passengers—especially during delays, storms, or mechanical snafus. Who hasn't seen the reverse of Kevin's facial adjustment, when an outbound flight to a premier destination is suddenly and definitively cancelled? Passengers can go from grinning to groaning in an instant, at the announcement of a cancelled flight. Just think how so many ordinary and yet personally intense stories can hinge on that one word proffered by the airport: CANCELLED. This is all part of the secret life of airports. It's a secret hidden in plain sight, of course. It's what makes airports legible spaces and what opens them up to mystery and narrativization in the first place: inescapable nonlinearity set against the otherwise linear patterns and rhythms of airport life.

Let's switch film examples, to see this in another context: When in *Toy Story 2* we arrive at the Tri-County International Airport for the climax of the movie, we know what to expect. We know how to read all the banal details of this generic place. Consider the realism within the initial approach shot. We know exactly how to decode the swooping curve of the terminal awning, at the curb; we understand the monolithic function of the air traffic control tower; we recognize the thunder of jets just above as they come in for landing, and the corollary energy they bestow; we have internalized the romantic cloudscapes that airport vistas afford. All these things in an instant—and once again, before our main characters are even in the picture.

By the time we follow Buzz Lightyear and company into the airport and beyond the check-in counter, we are already primed for the inner secrets of these sites. Namely, we find ourselves in a hyperreal, Escher-like labyrinth of the checked baggage system. Watching *Toy Story 2* with Julien, when we got to this scene, he asked in disbelief, "Is that what *really happens* to people's bags?" I remember equivocating, saying something like, "Well, sort of, but not *really*." For all the realism of the opening shot of Tri-County International Airport, it's important for this particular scene that the movie be a *Pixar* film, to allow for the reality of baggage makeup to become exaggerated, made into a spectacle worthy of a Christopher Nolan landscape, like something out of *Inception*. Recall those wrapped cityscapes and vertiginous hotel interiors, surreal Anthropocene nightmares that they were.

Curiously, the closing scene of *Inception* actually ends with a histrionic airport scene. Nolan treats the terminal with stark realism: nothing is warped or dreamlike in the airport, in that film. Whereas *Toy Story 2* exploits the hyperreal imaginary of airports, and *Home Alone 2* plays on the emotional spectrum of the site, *Inception* simply reaffirms the ordinary, mundane, and comfortingly *grounded* spatiality of airports. Is the secret life of airports explained better by their inner mysteries or by their sheer ordinariness? Or, is the secret life of airports somehow about precisely this tension, and specifically as it relates to watching movies? We cannot separate the Anthropocene from the cinematic imaginary, no matter how we value the aesthetic contributions therein.

Interestingly, several airports have taken to screening films for waiting passengers, to make the airport spaces more comfortable and entertaining, in and of themselves. The most remarkable example of this might be an outdoor movie screening that took place regularly during the summers on a concourse rooftop at the Dusseldorf airport in Germany.

The travel journalist Harriet Baskas once wrote an article for *USA Today* about trends involving airport cinemas, from Portland, Oregon to Singapore. The idea is that idle passengers and airline employees on break can effectively kill time by watching movies while at the airport. I saw one of these embedded theaters in the Minneapolis airport not long before Baskas wrote her piece. The mysterious new space was set off from the sprawling C concourse. There were some informational signs stating its mission: It was part of a local art project that sought to bring short films into the terminal for waiting passengers' viewing pleasure. When I stepped into the room I was struck by rows of comfortable seating and soft lighting. An edgy-looking documentary played on a large white wall that served as a screen. A motley crew of airline employees on break and bored travelers reposed in the seats while checking their phones, zoning out and relishing the quiet space—all the while completely misusing it. The art was not working, at least not as it was intended to work.

Airport movie theaters sound like a good idea in theory. Short films, video art pieces, and documentaries would be appropriate, so passengers won't have to commit too much time to emotional investment in narrative. Comfortable seating is obviously a draw. The danger, curiously, is that a *too* successful airport movie theater might keep passengers from making their flights on time and could detain airline employees in when they should be issuing boarding passes or deicing planes. Imagine a shrouded spectacle so enthralling that you'd settle in, lose track of time, and would never want to leave. Final boarding calls are made, but you don't even hear them … the cinema experience is too absorbing—*Infinite Jest* has become an airport. This is the challenge that airports striving to be hip will always face: how to keep traffic moving while yet attempting to be destinations themselves. Airport movie theaters compound this problem, promising high-value entertainment while risking the entire enterprise in motion. If airports actually became places where we would *choose* to linger, terminals at large may begin to resemble the airport in *World War Z*, thronging masses rushing toward the non-place. No, airports need you to want to get *out*, far away from them. This is part of their secret. And part of the dark truth of the Anthropocene—as if you can outrun your own impact on this life.

Here's where we can find a clue: on the safety briefing cards found in seatback pockets of commercial airliners. What do you see on these ostensibly innocuous, purely informational documents? You see the usual diagrams. How to don the oxygen mask (adults first, then your kids) and how to open the emergency exits. And these visual texts are hilarious if looked at with the slightest eye for comedy. The facial expressions of the oxygen-starved seatmates, the resigned march of evacuating passengers, the apparel worn by various passengers … . Julien often spends the minutes before takeoff reading these things as if they are short comic books. But next time you look at one of these cards, I want you to zoom in on one common frame in particular. It's on nearly every safety briefing card, where the emergency exit door is shown. Look at what is lying outside the emergency exit door, after a crash-landing: It's usually a place of pure green—even *greener*, to recall Vin Nardizzi's contribution to *Prismatic Ecology*.

What is that place? What is this great outdoors, this pristine landscape beneath a cerulean sky? Where exactly have we crashed, in this hypothetical scenario? It is a common theme. On one safety briefing card, available on Delta aircraft all over the country as I finish this book, the area outside the airplane is a radiant green field—no details, but verdantly idealized all the same. What is this place being fantasized about, at the end of these emergency escape slides?

A contemporaneous United Airlines safety briefing card clarifies this vision. On a similar frame, we see a little grass added into this place—as if to convince us that it's the real deal, *The Great Outdoors*. As if the Anthropocene never happened. Or if we could fly to a place outside of the polluted planet on which we live. It's a trope, all right—but what is it turning fliers toward? Is this the same place that was promised to fliers many decades ago, when major new airports were built, with a fecund paradise surrounding the runways? Is it outdated, or proof of an imagined future to come?

A promotional advertisement from 1980 for Atlanta's then new terminal showed a lush environment overflowing just beyond the airfield—layers and layers of green trees stretching out to the horizon. In this ad, travelers might as well have been flying in and out of paradise. The advertised airport is a natural place, full of opportunity, where every second counts. And yet, airports have to sustain their status as attractive transition zones, but only insofar as they keep people moving, out and away, to more *valuable* time. Thus the fecund greenery outlying the existence of the 1980s ATL, beckoning us to leave the bustle and flow of airport life for a more natural order of things. Of course, it doesn't always have to be *green* out there. As in *Home Alone 2*, it could just as easily be the seductive skyline of New York City, saying, "Come hither." Or a poinsettia on the desk, whispering *nature* (or maybe more accurately, borrowing from Donna Haraway's *When Species Meet*, "naturecultures": the whole bundle in and outside and shot through). But the point is this: the airport is only as good as it urges you to *leave*.

Sometimes when I tell people that I study airports, they'll say, "That must be a real niche!" But the truth is that airports are such a general, dispersed topic that it really isn't a niche at all. Nearly everyone has something to say about airports or air travel—even if it is just a story of a bad trip or a bizarre seatmate. We're all sort of specialists when it comes to flight—or we're invited to be, anyway. And as the opening clip from *Home Alone 2* suggests, airports communicate in such a common visual, dramatic, and comic language that just a brief scene staged in an airport can conjure a cluster of affects, sensations, and reversals. We interpret these things on the fly, as it were, and don't even realize we're doing it. It is for these reasons, among others, that I teach a class called Interpreting Airports: everyone comes in with way more background knowledge than they even knew they had. And airports measure our involvement with the Anthropocene, whether or not we want to admit it.

One time I mentioned to a bookseller that I was an author, and she asked what I wrote: "Fiction? Novels?" I said, no, I write about airports. She looked at me with a puzzled expression and remarked, "Oh, that must be boring." But even here in this strange response lies a kind of operative knowledge about what these spaces are, how they function, and what they feel like. *Boring.* In the mind, into the earth. The secret life of airports is a secret that many of us know, even if we don't know we know it.

And like so many topics these days, the secret life of airports comes back to Donald Trump and this age of post-truth, a stratigraphic blip in the Anthropocene. Recall how Trump castigated US airports in the first presidential debate, comparing them to those in "third-world countries" (or maybe comparing the airports *themselves* to third-world countries—it was a little unclear). Throughout his presidential campaign Trump repeatedly expressed a desire to improve airports across the country, to make them "tremendous." In a *Washington Times* article, Trump said "we have an obsolete plane system. We have obsolete airports. [...] We want the traveling public to have the greatest customer service and with an absolute minimum of delays." This sounded reasonable and even perhaps desirable, but how did Trump's bombastic vision sync with the secret life of airports? Is it fair to say that our airplanes are "obsolete?" I flew on two different planes the day before I wrote this, and both aircraft seemed to work just fine. Likewise, airports may be clunky and frustrating at times—but isn't that a necessary part of their design, as they facilitate the myriad nonlinear vectors and accommodate the millions of chaotic moving parts that make air travel on an international level possible in the first place? And if there are things to fix at these places, they have more to do with problems like structural racism and economic inequality, and less to do with simply streamlining the system. Airports may seem like an easy matter from the hallowed vantage point of a private jet or Air Force One, but we know that these places are very different on the ground, complex and messy zones with inherent tensions—places where, as a *Wall Street Journal* article put it in early 2017, "a Single Failed Router Can Ground a Thousand Flights."

Trump's mythic American airports of the future should have been a red flag for us, as we know that it's just not this simple—in the terminal, in a democratic republic, or in the Anthropocene. In fact, airports *rely* on their uneven qualities, their ups and downs. They are also not immune to the cumulative impression that air travel makes on the planet. And as airports stood in for Trump's notion of American progress in general as "a disaster," something to be whipped into shape once and for all and made Great, if we are to take airports seriously as a metonymy for culture at large, then we should be ready to admit that there is no easy fix, no final solution to the improvement of airports. Sure: Airports could conceivably get a little better, more efficient, more "user-friendly," as they say. And they probably will get incrementally better. But airports will always be airports, just like a democracy will always—one can hope—be a democracy: sometimes slow, but hopefully always for the better. And the Anthropocene will be the Anthropocene, as long as humans ignore it, or until humans really act differently toward the planet, on a massive scale.

Next time you find yourself trudging down a dank tunnel that seems to lead to nowhere, in the nether regions of an airport, suddenly alone and perhaps feeling a bit of existential dread, or maybe just exhaustion and boredom—remember that you are taking part in the secret life of airports. You're in the beating heart of the Anthropocene. These nonsimple spaces are indices for our broader culture, sites to interact with and interpret—sites that can make us feel exhilarated or stranded, by turns. This is what I call *airportness*, and it spreads out into all sorts of surprising things and seeps into unexpected places. It runs out everywhere, throughout our entire species at this point.

Airports can be used to propel entire stories, from *Home Alone 2* and *Toy Story 2* to Make America Great Again. But with their narrative potential comes all the other parts of textuality, as well: the ambiguities, the uncertainties, and the tensions. And all the other ecological implications, too: the exhaust, the waste, the forgetting about place. The secret life of airports is brimming with these things, and there's no escaping them. It's one thing to imagine effortless transitions from one place to another; it's quite another thing to fully inhabit these spaces, these awkward times on earth, and be conscious of them—aware that this is us, this is the pinnacle of mobility, human progress in the making, at least for now.

All That Is Solid Melts into Airports

A Bloomberg article in the summer of 2017 declared: "The Airports of the Future Are Here."

Never mind the temporal contradiction in the headline—I was intrigued. I started reading the article and almost immediately decided to assign it in my Interpreting Airports Honors seminar at Loyola. The article highlights several top-rated airports around the world and suggests that innovations just on the horizon will make future airports easier to navigate and more efficient. New biometric scanning equipment is lauded, and these same technologies are predicted to revamp the routines of bag drop, security, and customs. I breezed through the piece (it's maybe a thousand words, max), rolled my eyes at a few points, then set it aside.

When I revisited this clickbait piece with my students, I was astounded by how oddities and insidious assumptions crept up throughout. Had I never reread this throwaway article, it would have been lost in the oblivion of online news, another garbage instance of futurism intended only to drive internet advertising in the moment. But not this time. My students and I sunk into this piece. We read it closely, using the assorted tools that liberal arts critics learn to carry and deploy at will. And it was incredibly illuminating.

This class is an interdisciplinary seminar, meaning, truth be told, a *loosely* disciplinary seminar. I'm an English professor, but the class barely resembles an "English" class per se. My students and I consider a wide variety of things in this seminar, from popular business-themed articles to ethnographies, from historical accounts to visual art, from poems to architectural master plans. Little do they know that they are also studying the Anthropocene—until, from time to time, it bursts into full view. Throughout our class we're talking about air travel and its discontents—unpacking the baggage, as it were, of our culture of flight. The Bloomberg article was readymade for us. In fact, I depend on such serendipitous texts to be the required reading of my courses.

In the first paragraph of the piece in question, something literary jumped out at us immediately: "Transiting a modern hub such as Munich or Seoul is more easily endured than threading your way through the perpetual construction zones that pass for airports around New York." What are these *perpetual construction zones*? My students were quick to jump on this: they are *metaphors*! When talking about airports, even in a frank, business-forward fashion, it's as if we can't avoid heading into literary land: a realm of fantasy and fabulation, poetry and fiction. Even when airports *include* areas under renovation, it is a stretch to say that they *are* construction zones. Or is it?

Many airports *are* construction zones, even as they continue to operate normally on a day-to-day basis: getting people from curb to plane, from plane to plane, and plane to curb. Even as they do these things, airports are under renovation and sometimes outright rebuilding. At my home airport just outside New Orleans, a new terminal is being built across the runway. The existing structure increasingly feels dilapidated and abject as gates are phased out in anticipation of the new space in progress: a skein of columns and beams, plate glass windows, massive skeletal arcades—a billion-dollar project not quite legible, yet, as an airport.

So the construction zone is a metaphor that contains kernels of truth, especially as we consider the theme of the Bloomberg piece, *airports of the future*. Readers are primed for the future by this derogatory metaphor. If we start thinking about airports as part-rubble, half-built, then maybe we can better steel ourselves to imagine the airports to come. Even as the world threatens to crumble around these illustrious fields.

What are these airports, what promises do they hold? What secrets do they hide? The Bloomberg piece gets more interesting as we read on. With a widening array of amenities and entertainment options—not to mention employment opportunities—"People will *choose* to go to the airport." This is a recurring fantasy fruit that gets juiced from time to time: the idea that airports may become so desirous as to become destinations themselves. But there is always a threshold here, at which point people decide that their present space takes priority over far-flung locales. If the ultimate airport is a rich, luscious place brimming with entrainment and energy, a true magnet for local citizens—and if every airport can become such a site—of what use are the airplanes, of what use the term "destination" as we know it? Business futurist John Kasarda has called these projected future nodes *aerotropoli*, but we might as well ground the pesky planes and call such a place utopia, instead.

In the next paragraph of the Bloomberg piece, things get even more interesting. We learn about "infrastructure investments and technologies that will, in theory, allow airports to largely eradicate the dreaded waiting." *In theory*. Of course, we all know that the *practice* of air travel is far messier and more uncomfortable than the airline loyalty pamphlets or ad spots make it appear. Indeed, the "dreaded waiting" acts as an instance of apophasis in this sentence, stating and projecting the very thing that is supposedly being put under erasure. But another word stands out here: "eradicate." I ask my students what contexts this word evokes, and they say *disease*, *insects*, and *pests*. Look how the phenomenology of airport waiting gets *naturalized* as something that can be cast out—as if once and for all. Yet we know the truth of the matter is that any number of factors out of any one person's direct control—weather, technology, geopolitics, human psychology—can snarl air travel and make it grind to a halt. The *in theory* collapses under even the most minimal invitation of texture and details—under the reality of flight as a hallmark of the Anthropocene.

The same paragraph explains how "travelers will migrate around the terminal faster and see fewer walls and physical barriers." Here is another naturalizing word, "migrate"—as if admitting the wild, undomesticated, nonlinear status of human travelers as a creaturely *species*. And again the civilized portrait of the hallowed future of airports shatters into a variegated, ragged landscape with beasts run amok. As if to drive this image home, the final sentence of this paragraph includes the clause "how airports will evolve"—suddenly, airports themselves are changing organisms in an ecosystem unfolding over time. There might as well be a sentence to follow about how airports are an undeniable feature of the Anthropocene.

The tension between a naturalist imaginary and cultural progress grows. Later in the article an aviation industry leader states, "We need to evolve the terminals into being little cities." It's a strange way to think about evolution, as an active verb, as something that humans can *do* to other things (like airports). Either way, to talk in terms of evolution is to conjure vast expanses of time. This is hardly consistent with the temporal framework of this piece, which is focused on the next two to three decades, at most. How airports "will evolve" may sound like an edgy way to talk about air travel—but are we really prepared to consider human flight on an evolutionary timescale? The actual edge here is precipitous.

The next paragraph commences with a bold pronouncement: "One day, the airport will know 'everything about everyone moving in the airport,' said Seth Young, director of the Center for Aviation Studies at Ohio State University." My students rightly identify this as a horrific situation: a society of total surveillance in which everyone is free as long as everyone is constantly monitored and anyone can be eliminated from the system at any moment. Quite the picture of democratic mobility, a constantly patrolled garden of earthly delights.

Further down the rabbit hole we go. My students bristle when we read that as part of the process, an airport design firm "measured anxiety levels for different passenger types." My students want details. They want to know how exactly anxiety can be measured—particularly given the squishy, subjective reality of anxiety, which, as many of them attest, only gets heightened when it is being *measured*. Furthermore, what is a passenger *type*? My students pounce on this sentence, and I gleefully urge them on. What sounds like justifiable social science in the service of good design buckles under the slightest humanistic scrutiny. This is not what we should call human progress. But like it or not, it is the Anthropocene running at full tilt.

The Bloomberg piece drives toward an unsurprising endpoint: how airports are, fundamentally, revenue-generating machines. "Amid all this increased efficiency, airports are also keen to have people linger so they'll buy more stuff." My students are rattled by the unflappable admission that the romantic, cosmopolitan miracle of flight is really no more than a thinly veiled excuse for rampant consumerism and profit extraction. The airport-as-mall is a well-trod expression, but the article makes it quite literal:

> "The number of passengers that flow through airports really rivals any other mechanism out there that can congregate that many customers in one place," says Ken Buchanan, executive vice president of revenue management for Dallas-Fort Worth International, the fourth-largest U.S. airport by passenger numbers. "It's like having a Super Bowl worth of people every single day."

The airport is a *mechanism* that *congregates customers*. Somehow we have stumbled into the murky depths of almost Marxian-sounding language, where people are transformed mechanistically, but also religiously, into self-alienated units of production: the production of money. As if we needed this reinforced, the Super Bowl appears ambiguously as a figure of revenue generation and also of mass entertainment and spectation. The airport becomes a fixture of the home, an economic force, once again weirdly naturalized, even as it's strange, fundamental relationship to money is laid bare. We had set out to read about and discuss cutting-edge airport *design*: adjustments and attunements to the phenomenology of air travel. Instead, it all comes down to padding the pockets of owners and executives, at the expense of the plodding masses who fly (and spend) or work (and spend) in order to keep the immense, ambiguous structure intact. And it's a place clearly under stress—so the Anthropocene becomes metonymically apparent.

The next paragraph describes travelers as a "captive audience," a phrase that strikes us as ominous given the high-security sensitivity of these spaces. These vying metaphors—captivity, entertainment, religiosity, finance—simultaneously distract from the primary subject of flight and explain its twisted underlying logic. The contemporary airport is completely unsure of what it is, and how it got here.

Marx once described the juggernaut of capitalism in terms of a "constant revolutionizing of production"—a process wherein "all that is solid melts into air" (617). In this article about airport futurism, Marx's famous expression comes to life. In a passage of the Bloomberg article about the imminent rise in autonomous vehicles, a concern is expressed that this alternative mode of transit "will siphon off a chunk of shorter flights that are 500 miles or less." Consider the intricate alchemy here: flights (air travel) converted into solid "chunks" only to be siphoned (as a liquid) into ground transit. *All that is solid melts into airports*—or into some form of chimerical passage, anyway. The bit about autonomous vehicles is cashed out as such: "For U.S. airports, the ascension of self-driving cars will create a costly conundrum: how to replace parking revenue, which typically represents a quarter of annual airport budgets." *Creating a costly conundrum*: it almost sounds like poetry. And indeed, humans are all but eliminated from this airport picture. What matters is the bottom line: costs, revenues, budgets, profits.

This is, of course, no real surprise, and hardly unique: The airport is another mere point of potential growth within the ongoing sprawl of consumer culture. But there's something extraordinary happening here, something about the peculiar tensions between humanist pursuits (togetherness, connection, communication) and the boldfaced nature of impersonal capitalist hegemony at work around airport futurism. It is the apotheosis of the Anthropocene.

I may be starting to sound like a stereotypical, radical leftist Marxist English professor, influencing my innocent students and corrupting their minds. Two defenses: First, my own college education happened at Hillsdale College, a bastion of free market libertarianism and conservative politics; Hillsdale is where I first learned to read closely for economic dynamics (if not exactly with the intended grain, here). Second, my students guided me to at least half of the epiphanies in the present Bloomberg article. And these epiphanies took place right on the surface: we were not "reading into" this piece. It's all right there; look at the next paragraph:

> To find new revenue, airport executives will need to attract dollars in other ways, via dining, shopping, and entertainment. Since that may not be enough, new business models will be needed for ground transportation and commercial office space; perhaps new revenue may accrue from baggage delivery service.

This has almost nothing to do with the feel of airports, the architecture of travel, or the experience of being a human body in flight. It is precisely about "airport executives" attracting dollars. *Baggage* here isn't your or my actual luggage; it's just another means to generate revenue for the airport executive.

As if this were not enough, we go on to learn that "At Changi, concession revenues rose 5 percent last year to a record $1.6 billion, while the world's busiest airport, Atlanta's Hartsfield-Jackson International, topped $1 billion in concession sales in 2016, also a record." Such statements show how global capitalism entices its human actants into being surprised by setting ever new records of accumulation—when this is in fact exactly what global capitalism sets out to *do*, how it *works*. Global capitalism sets out to accumulate ever more surplus value, and then surprises itself by doing this very thing to ever-greater degrees, breaking new records every year. The whole process is thereby naturalized as an organic, spontaneous eruption. It's evolution, baby.

The penultimate paragraph of the Bloomberg article elicits strong skepticism from my students:

> "Our efforts to grow Changi's commercial business and provide an enjoyable shopping and dining experience is part and parcel of enhancing the overall airport experience for our passengers, and will continue in the years to come," the airport said in an emailed statement.

Now that we've seen the true inner workings of airport futurism, how are we supposed to believe for one second that this is about "enhancing the overall airport experience for our passengers"? My students scoffed at this insincere claim. And wait: who even "said" this, anyway? *The airport*. The airport *emailed* the statement. All that is solid melts into airports—airports that can e-mail.

This animation of the airport continues:

> "No matter what," Young said, "airports want to make it efficient." That means getting through quickly—be it arriving, departing, or transferring. "But they love it when people are at the airport," he added, "because of the opportunities to spend money."

Airports *want*. They desire. But do they actually want what Young (director of the Center for Aviation Studies at Ohio State University) says they want? Not at all. Airports *love* it when travelers are stuck, when efficiency breaks down—so that people will "spend money." The Bloomberg article spirals into a mind-bending chasm where airports lumber around wanting and loving, and people are hapless embodied bank accounts being shuttled to and fro. The utopia of airports in the future has decidedly turned into a dystopia of the ongoing present: an Anthropocene sinkhole.

This all might sound preposterous. My class spent a full week on this article. I tell my students the point of such an exercise—well, it isn't an *exercise* at all—is to slow down and read closely what we are not supposed to. This sort of article is intended for quick digestion and internalization. Normalization. But I'm showing my students how to stick with something that asks to be disposed of quickly, in good Anthropocene fashion. I've stuck with airports and air travel for over fifteen years now—writing, thinking, teaching, critiquing—and I'm more intrigued and baffled by these spaces than ever. We know that commercial airlines are unflappable about their reliance on a strict class system: they brazenly call certain people "Elite" while relegating others to "Economy," and even "Basic Economy," now! This is a not so subtle dig at the true *base* of this whole enterprise. And when we project this normalized state of affairs out into the near future, what do we see? This is not my beautiful terminal.

Airports of the future? Sure, makes total sense. Common sense. But airports as animate, appetitive agents who feed off the paltry incomes of petit bourgeoisies, only to metastasize and grow larger and larger, biometric scanning bodies who read and consume people, only in order to grow their own tumorous tendrils and limbs? Jetways extending upon jetways, shop-laden terminals leading to nowhere while operating like gigantic ATMs? What Ozymandian future are we building, here? Is this the future we will choose, as the makers of airplanes and airports? It doesn't have to be. But for it not to be, we need to acknowledge our complicity in this, and disentangle the strong threads of capitalist fantasy woven around our airports as they are, and as we plod forward into our as yet uncertain future, as a very real species partaking in evolution on this planet that is, itself, airborne.

Engine Failure

"Falcon Heavy, in a Roar of Thunder, Carries SpaceX's Ambition Into Orbit." So reads a *New York Times* headline on the biggest spectacle of the week in early 2018. Elon Musk's latest rocket blasted into the atmosphere with David Bowie's iconic "Space Oddity" playing on auto-repeat, listened to by no one. Crowds cheered as the rocket roared upon takeoff—carrying a Tesla Roadster as payload, no less—and roared again as two of the boosters delivered themselves safely back to Earth.

The sound of jet propulsion can be both mesmerizing and forgettable. As such, it's also a constant reminder of the Anthropocene.

One time, in my room on the fourteenth floor of the Watergate Hotel during a visit to Washington, DC, I became distinctly aware of a succession of rumbles in the sky each early morning: the steady sounds of the first banks of commercial airliners taking off from Reagan airport, across the Potomac. This is nothing out of the ordinary. A faint, increasing thunder, then a gradual sonic wane as twin turbofans churn the outside air into propellant thrust, and an airliner ascends after takeoff.

It might seem silly to even remark on it. This happens to me more often than I'd like to admit: I'll hear a jet rumbling above, and gaze up and say "Wow!"—and whoever I'm with stares at me like I'm some sort of Neanderthal. But this dull roar denotes a truly astonishing feat happening each and every day, on regular and tight schedules. These are the workhorses of the sky, transporting people and cargo around the planet for labor and leisure, the grinds of work and duty commingling with the fantasies of vacation and pleasure. Turbofans propel both bodies and box shipments around the globe. Yet here's what's weird: The same technologies that quite literally thrust people and things into space and the future are also the very things that might be holding humans back from truly radical, forward-looking innovations.

Throughout 2017 there was considerable technology buzz about new developments in electric turbofan engines. This advancement would result in a quieter, more fuel-efficient mode of jet propulsion—and thereby a cheaper and less-polluting form of air travel. Promotional spots for the products often show energy diagrams with bold green arrows and lines, or sleek aircraft soaring above verdant, rolling landscapes. Rolls Royce, for instance, is collaborating with Siemens and Airbus to develop a hybrid-electric technology aircraft on which one of the four gas turbine engines—a turbofan painted green—will be powered solely by electric energy. The idea is that the plane will have three normal gas turbofans as backup as they test the green engine for stress, safety, and reliability. The goal is to fly this test plane by 2020, suggesting that the technology could conceivably be put into use within the next couple decades.

The aircraft model for this particular test plane is a British Aerospace 146 (BAE-146). The BAE-146 is a smallish, short- to mid-range aircraft most commonly used for regional routes (70 to 112 seats, depending on the configuration). It's a distinctive plane, resembling a miniature cargo jet with a high-wing cantilever design and four comparatively small engines. This is a rather old plane, first flown in 1981 and no longer in commercial service in the United States. As of this writing, only 144 of the 387 aircraft built are still in operation around the world. In other words, the green engine testing is not being conducted on a mainstream airframe—the type of plane where the real money is for airlines as well as aircraft and turbofan manufacturers. Instead, an obsolescing aircraft is being used to test out new propulsion technology. It's an investment in green energy, then, but perhaps more symbolic than realistic in terms of widespread, cost-effective use.

At the same time, larger-scale equipment is also undergoing renewal and innovation. Rolls Royce is developing a new power gearbox that will result in 25 percent greater fuel efficiency in their large turbofans by 2025, relative to the 20-year-old Trent 700 model. Regarding their newer Trent 7000 turbofans, designed for the wide-body Airbus A330neo (250 to 400 passengers), Rolls Royce confidently claims that these engines are "Future-proofed on noise and emissions, with plenty of margin against both current and future environmental targets/legislation." Consider this statement for a moment. This turbofan has apparently been designed to meet future demands and regulations corresponding to various types of pollution. This both assumes a worsening state of affairs (more air traffic congestion, greater ecological urgency, etc.), and it assures buyers that these things have already been planned for and built into the engine. It amounts to copping to the tragedy of what's coming, and then congratulating oneself for being so ready for it. It is a curious way to think about the future, if you pause to contemplate it.

And certainly, even as turbofan and aircraft manufacturers alike make appeals to cleaner technology, their goal is *not* to reduce human air travel. Regarding its A330 model, at the time of this writing Airbus charts 1,694 orders for these planes, of which 1,373 are fulfilled and 321 are in "backlog." The implicit message: demand has not been met, which means building more planes, and faster. And this is presented as an ongoing condition. An airline manufacturer would never aim to satisfy the needs of all airlines once and for all, but rather to keep producing new jets *ad infinitum*. So even if the planes to come are powered by relatively cleaner Trent 7000 turbofans, the assumption—and the *goal*—is to put ever more A330s in the sky. That somewhat complicates the straightforward aim of hitting "environmental targets," as Rolls Royce puts it. Individually, sure—but collectively, if more planes are in the sky? A typical Anthropocene blind spot.

Aviation futurists might argue that as old planes are retired the newer, more efficient aircraft will simply replace these, and that consolidation will reduce overall flights and eliminate unnecessary routes. Yet it is clear that Airbus and Boeing are hardly going to turn away new business or slow down production. Consider how Airbus boldly claims on their website that their A320 family is the "world's best-selling aircraft of all time"; and then look at how Boeing, on their website, shows off a cornucopia of customers for their comparable next-generation 737 planes (a projection complicated by the time that I am finishing this book). This is obviously a race for *growth*, not just efficiency.

Turbofan engines offer an audible reminder of the paradox of progress. As much as people may want to experience new things, they have to use old tools and means to do so. Sometimes those tools and means can function as blinders. People are tied to existing patterns, infrastructure, and systems even as they might want or need to move forward, to do something different and truly innovative.

Leaving DC at the end of my trip, I was struck by the beauty of Eero Saarinen's Dulles airport at dawn. Approaching the terminal from the highway, if you take the time to look, it's a truly remarkable building. The way it sweeps up from the ground, how it architecturally announces the grand project of flight … . It feels like a paean to the jet age, a living monument of sorts. The interior is no less striking, with its impressive vaulted ceiling and structural elements in full view above.

As I plodded through the security checkpoint slog and onward to my gate, however, it occurred to me how stuck travelers are in this bizarre moment of the past, this mid-twentieth-century endeavor that is jet travel. Innovations in turbofan engine design and technology may be well-intentioned and forward-thinking, at least in some sense. And the actual work that turbofans do day in and day out, hour after hour of nonstop chugging across the sky … it's nothing less than incredible, from a technical standpoint. But, at the same time, the din of flight really can't help but remind people of something that had its heyday several decades ago—and something that has taken a significant toll on the planet.

The bitter truth is that human air travel probably won't get much better in the years to come. It might have reached certain limits in terms of speed, economy, and comfort. There are any number of signs that this is the case: climate change, limited resources, land-use constraints, wealth inequality, and so on. Air travel is *not* immune to the larger problems of the Anthropocene.

In late 2017, news broke about problems in the Rolls Royce Trent 1000 engines that power the Boeing 787, which was first introduced in 2011: The turbine blades on two separate aircraft broke down during flight, resulting in severe vibrations and causing the aircraft to abort their journeys. Concerning these incidents, Rolls Royce chief executive Warren East admitted an obvious but uncomfortable truth about turbofan parts: "They wear out."

For all of Elon Musk's bluster, and even granting the incredible engineering brilliance behind SpaceX's accomplishments, an odd detail slipped into one of Musk's presentations on "making life multiplanetary." The pressurized area of the payload section of his planned Mars spaceship is described as being "greater than the cabin of an Airbus A380." The fact is meant to be impressive, but it doesn't quite square with the expected duration of the trip to Mars. Three to six months traveling in a super jumbo jet? No thanks. 16 hours in an A380 can already drive one to the point of insanity, no matter how luxurious the accommodations. And incidentally, the A380 program would be cancelled within a year of this announcement, making the comparison even less charming. In a similar rhetorical move, the mass of Musk's star rocket, the Falcon Heavy, has been explained by comparison to a 737—the most widely used Boeing commercial airliner in service today. To envision a reusable space rocket as little more than a vertically aligned Southwest plane brings the stars down to earth indeed. The ambitions and technological marvels of Musk's rockets are weighed down by the twentieth-century baggage of commercial flight.

For now, the goal of human air travel seems to be to keep it going at any cost—as if humanity is still headed somewhere else, somewhere new. Rolls Royce plans to "power the aircraft of the future," as a company statement boldly puts it. And SpaceX is certainly working hard to produce another aspect of this future. But is the future in play here truly something revolutionary? Whether encapsulated in the dreams of a billionaire technologist or nestled in the gear teeth of a "next-generation" turbofan, the roar of the future gets awkwardly dampened. It sounds a lot like the present, or maybe even more like the past. Understood this way, it makes perverse sense why Musk sent a car into outer space, going nowhere, as if to consecrate once and for all the twentieth century as a final frontier, or the strangely retroactive apex of the Anthropocene.

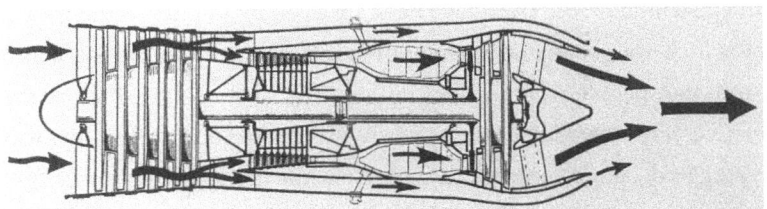

Figure 4 *A simple diagram of a jet engine belies the Anthropocene.*

Wheels in the Sky

We often look for evidence of the Anthropocene on the terrestrial ground or high up in the atmosphere; around other species' populations or somewhere in the ocean. But as I'm hoping to show, the Anthropocene also has an elusive yet ongoing connection to human flight. As yet one more example of this, consider the enduring fantasy of flying cars. It's a reoccurring motif: every year or so it seems like I read the same article about how flying cars are *just about* to take flight. They used to mimic coupes, but lately they have come to resemble enlarged hobby drones. Whatever is fashionable to people on the ground is projected as eventually (but very soon!) carrying them into the air.

Despite the hype, such articles tend to reinforce the idea that flying cars belong in science fiction rather than on Earth. A September 2017 article in the *Guardian* on flying cars couldn't help but reference both Luke Skywalker's landspeeder and *Back to the Future* within the first two paragraphs. Another more recent *New York Times* article cautioned that while flying taxis were probably still years away, the "groundwork is accelerating." This strange description suggests a frantic substructural race to become airborne, as if humans had never flown before—as if our planet weren't itself already spinning in space.

Meanwhile ordinary cars on the ground are facing something of an existential crisis. They have been usurped by phones as the means by which we project an image of ourselves, and it seems more and more that people would rather be scrolling than driving. Picture the furtive, scrambled look on the face of the driver you last saw who was trying to do something on their phone while driving. They are caught between contradictory embodiments of cellular agency and an older form of individual freedom.

At the same time, climate change threatens to flood cities and render automobiles useless at worst and insurance claim headaches at best. Hurricanes sweep through coastal cities, and news images show stranded SUVs and waterlogged sedans. Our cars no longer promise safe passage, much less sure escape routes. Car manufacturers continue to churn out new models and find clever ways to market them. But our fatal attachment to these things is showing signs of strain.

Take a commercial for the Volkswagen Tiguan that was circulating around the internet and on television in early 2018, which features an apparently well-off white couple frantically loading their car to evacuate what the TV proclaims as a "METEOR HEADING TOWARD METRO AREA." The disjunctive tone of this commercial, which seemed eerily prophetic against the backdrop of Kim Jong Un's almost contemporaneous missile launches, is a bit bewildering—part whimsy, part despair. As the couple loads bottled water and a laundry basket into the back of their chili-pepper-red SUV, the wifely figure shouts, "We can fit more!" and the ad cuts to the husband ripping a TV off the wall. A distant flash lights the suburban hillsides in an eerie orange glow. Eventually the Tiguan is turned on, and for a split second all we see are the dials and displays coming to life, as if we're in the cockpit of a spacecraft from *Star Wars*—if only this really were a flying car. Cut to a wide angle of the SUV as it is backed out of the driveway, and then the couple races on a smoothly flowing highway to party music as the fireball plummets, presumably about to change the world forever. This is a commercial for the Anthropocene if there ever was one.

Whatever is happening in the sky, an automobile is not going to save the day, no matter how deceptively spacious or spritely it is. Yet even as VW reveals consumerist accumulation as somewhat ironic as we linger on the brink of annihilation, VW continues also to try to sell vehicles with it—they let you carry everything with you, all your important personal property, over the brink.

It's as if car companies don't know what else to do. They can't devise an alternative to consumerism's eternal appeals to individualism, to personal choice and identity projection, even as these sit in stark contrast with the collective doom we face.

If the days of car culture are seen as numbered, it helps explain the search for ways to refresh their presence in our midst. Thus the Tiguan ad ironizes while continuing our current relationship to cars, and the news stories about flying cars keep us looking wistfully toward a future relationship with cars to come. These treatments of automobility place cars beyond the horizon of environmental or social critiques or condemnation, and maintain them in the realm of wonder and entertainment.

If the twentieth century championed the rise and democratization of the individual drive, the twenty-first century might signal the end of it. Around the same time that the Tiguan ad was subliminally suggesting North Korean missiles, another rocket was being prepared for launch—this one with an automobile in tow. In Florida on February 6, 2018, SpaceX launched the Falcon Heavy, the most powerful commercial rocket in operation, in the direction of Mars, with CEO Elon Musk's personal red Tesla aboard as the payload. Behind the wheel was a mannequin named Starman, steering the vehicle on its ultimate trajectory to the void. In a spectacle meant to foretell a trajectory for human survival involving space colonization, a $100,000 convertible has symbolically been relegated to mere space junk, on a drive to nowhere.

One way to read this spectacle is as a further diminishment of automobility's already faded promise. My friend Ian Bogost argued in a 2015 *Atlantic* article that Tesla was "acclimating us to the end of the automobile as an object of desire." Sending the car into space could be read as a metaphoric extension of that: the car is little more than an outmoded piece of trash, a cosmically cheap toy, an ornament for a form of transportation that now nourishes hope and promise. SpaceX ups the ante, flouting global catastrophe and going bigger than mere flying cars, in one exorbitant gesture.

But at the same time, the Falcon Heavy launch was also an epic car commercial for Musk's Tesla brand. In another *Atlantic* article, Marina Koren described the launch not only as a shrewd advertising ploy for Tesla but also for the commercialization of outer space and the new form of individualism expressed not in terms of what you drive but what you can personally put in orbit: "As commercial companies take bigger and bigger bites out of the industry, the business of spaceflight has become less universal, and more personal." Musk has become a trailblazer in transforming outer space not into habitable space but into ad space, ready to be populated with name brands.

Beginning with his own cast-off convertible, Musk has made space into junk space. Launching his sports car into space is less a celebration of car culture than a confirmation of cars as an emblem of selfishness rather than progress. Commercial space flight appears not as the future of humankind but the future of egotism. A Batman signal in space, but it reads *Anthropocene* instead—and no one is coming to the rescue.

A few weeks before the launch of the Falcon Heavy, a Dodge Ram commercial played during the Super Bowl that seemed on one level to counteract the selfishness of car culture, equating personal vehicles with self-sacrifice and civic progress. In the ad, Martin Luther King Jr. speaks in a voice-over about what it means to "serve," as a collage of images of volunteerism, social work, and military power flashes across the screen. Spliced into these snapshots of courage are three fairly generic clips of the Ram pickup: first as mere headlights; second in full force, splashing through mud; and finally rumbling directly toward the camera at eye level.

As in the Tiguan ad, this commercial presents contradictory messages as apparently cohesive, couching the sales pitch in the insouciant frisson of cognitive dissonance. The ad deploys King, an advocate and practitioner of nonviolent activism, to sanctify a soldier's poignant return from defending the US's interests abroad: The final scene shows a soldier in fatigues hugging a boy, presumably his son. And where are they reuniting? In an airport—iconic Eames tandem sling-seats lined beside them on both sides.

By evoking militarized scenes of crisis, the Dodge ad seems to cede that the world is becoming inescapably ridden with conflict. No more emphasis on the old staples of car and truck ads, in which romantic country roads and harmonious cityscapes ordain the screen. Instead the Ram becomes perceptible as a *Mad Max*-esque vehicle for salvaging the Anthropocene: In the ad, a gun case is loaded into a paramilitary helicopter; an injured dog is pulled from smoldering rubble; many men haul something up an icy cliff. Even though there are also clips of football games, children, and even an ultrasound probe roving over a pregnant belly, the ad's world seems to be trembling on the brink. King's words come across as all the more moving for how they seem to declare the twentieth century as definitively past. We are in a new moment where those words are little more than memory and marketing fodder.

Recently I received a marketing e-mail from Subaru announcing their latest model: the Ascent. The message invited me to "be the first to own the biggest Subaru SUV we've ever made." I couldn't help but detect a tone of desperation in this promotional junk mail. It touted Apple CarPlay, Android Auto integration, and Wi-Fi connectivity, as if trying to steal back some of the glamour from phones. *Be the first*: as if such a thing were possible, when whispered by spam. *The biggest*: as if that were a badge of honor, rather than shame. *Ascent*: as if this SUV is soaring ever upward, maybe even out into space to join the Tesla.

Yet the Ascent is really another plateau, more of the same—just with a slightly higher monthly payment.

Automobility has reached a crisis point, and somehow we're all too aware of it: the latest car ads scream it. Still sold to the masses as personalized dreams ready to come true, the reality is a nightmare we're already living, and it's called the Anthropocene. Despite Subaru's promises of Ascent and Buick's calls for Encore, it's hard not to take a slightly removed perspective and see an abused planet rotating in space, crisscrossed with tire tracks and littered with the detritus of individual drive.

First-Class Amenities

Leafing through the 2018 summer fiction issue of *The New Yorker*, an advertisement grabs my eye: it is awash in blinding light, so bright that it at first appears to be a printing mistake. But no, the ad depicts an airliner window in the background, the source and reason for the prodigious whiteness. This reminds me of a Twitter thread concerning the etiquette of shutting window shades on airliners: when they should be left open (and by whom, in each case) and when they should be closed (to keep the cabin cool, respect morning sleepers, etc.). Natural light in airliners is a contested subject, it turns out—if "natural" is the right word for sunlight experienced by human beings cruising at 36,000 feet.

"… AND RELAX"—so says the slogan across the tableaux of the ad, which shows a pair of eyeglasses laying upside down on an airline blanket, beside an unzipped pouch which appears to have spilt its contents onto the milky surface beneath: an eye mask, as well as two small tubes of lotion, and a miniscule bottle of something that says SPA, RELAX, and PULSE POINT. The amenity bag boasts in fine print that it has been produced by The White Company exclusively for British Airways. The wording below this scene reads: "A thoughtful Amenity Kit to take your mind off the world below. Your Club World. Our Business Class." *The world below*—is this the crumbling world of the Anthropocene?

For an ad about simplicity and relaxation, this is actually a lot of information to take in. The ad is making an obvious pitch for business class passengers to fly British Airways instead of the competition. Business class sections make up a critical part of the economic model of the premier transatlantic airlines, and every perceived perk matters when it comes to filling these seats. I long to dig deeper into the leather pouch in the ad, to see what else might be inside. Such grandiose promises for such a modest container—and, probably most of the time, disposed of at the end of long-haul flights. Knowing that British Airways fairly recently started offering 787 service directly from Heathrow to my home airport in New Orleans, I do a quick search for a one-week trip—departing and returning on Wednesdays, to keep the fare as low as possible—and confront a price tag of $8,943.12. I won't be taking this flight anytime soon, and certainly not just so I can do research into the tantalizing Amenity Kit. (The curious capitalization of this thing is enough to intrigue the eager cultural critic.) On the other hand, I've chatted with Mark Vanhoenacker periodically on Twitter; I'll bet he could score me one of these kits … .

It jogs my memory, though, and I recall a curious interaction I had with a neighbor a few weeks prior: Ron, my neighborhood all-around good guy and Airedale walker, had knocked on my door and said he had something for me; he held out a paper bag and I took it, feeling several odd shapes jostle around inside. "My church collects airline amenity kits and gives them to the local shelter. But, well, we had these 747 kits and I thought, since the 747 was in the news this week … well, maybe YOU should have these." The *New York Times* had just run a feature about the final flight of a Delta 747, the last US carrier to operate the iconic jumbo jets, to the desert boneyard where it will rest until its parts are needed to refurbish still operating 747s in other parts of the world.

Ron waved goodbye in his signature somewhat embarrassed fashion and walked down the block with his dog. I was standing there still processing the exchange, then I looked down into the bag: it was full of shrink-wrapped kits of various sizes, from several years of 747 business class service. As soon as Julien and Camille heard the sound of packaging they tore into the room and promptly pulled out several of the kits and ran off with them. I managed to hang on to a couple, and I badgered them away for future … something. Future proof that these things, 747s and all their postmodern oddities and opulence, existed. The iconic jumbo jet as some kind of indicator species of the Anthropocene.

Now, titillated by the British Airways ad, I rummage around my bottom desk drawer and pull one of the kits out. It's time to open it, and to see what these small vessels contain. The British Airways ad makes the Kit seem transcendental, utterly distinctive. How passé will the United kit seem, in comparison to these new (if only minimally evinced) Kits from British Airways? I won't be able to answer this question fully, as I cannot do a side-by-side assessment. Nevertheless, let me see what United offered to its equivalent business class customers. I tear it out of its plastic baggy, on which I learn that it was part of United's Polaris Business Class program.

The metal ovoid can displays a 747 profile from below, with four contrails trailing behind—as if to perversely announce *pollution, here we come*. Opening it up, I am immediately struck by just how much is packed inside. I cannot decipher any individual thing yet, only a cornucopia of wrappers and other materials—elastic, cotton, paper, plastic. I can see at least eight discrete objects inside. It is a grayscale Easter basket, in miniature. A survival kit for the late Anthropocene.

The first thing I pluck out of the matrix is a small, square paper coupon: 20 percent off my first purchase of b4 products, "A luxury hand sanitizer product with a cause." Already I feel spun out far beyond the business class cocoon seat and into a messier world of body creams and causes. I can't go on. I'll go on.

Earplugs in a cloudy wax paper wrapper. "Roll earplug; Insert into ear."

A small pen, 3-inches long. Very cute, but I can't imagine writing anything with it, nothing beyond half-drunk epiphanies after a gin and tonic at 36,000 feet. Or maybe the contact info of a similarly inebriated seatmate; even if courtesy curtains separate, seatmate bonds can happen. (Remember the infamous Brad Pitt business class seatmate discovery of 2015? This pen could have captured his signature, if that were a United flight.)

A toothbrush, crystal clear handle and nestled base. Distributed by Linstol, USA, LLC—Naples, FL. 34114. The pen didn't say where it came from. Personal hygiene, it would seem, warrants a firm origin. As if "distribution" equals a source. Yet we are all too widely distributed objects in the Anthropocene.

Cowshed lip balm, chamomile refreshing towelette, and restoring hand cream. Ah, hah! Something needs *restoring*. A subtle sign that something has gone wrong. (The b4 "causes" were more of an insinuation.) In this package is a *second* 20 percent off coupon, at the back of a booklet for these products from Soho & Co, a London-based "private members club." The booklet smells amazing—like lemon balm just purchased from a rustic, sought-after apothecary. This amenity kit goes far beyond the United experience aloft, and into a receding, metastasizing consumer-scape on the ground.

Then I pull out an absolute charm, a fantastically diminutive tube of Colgate toothpaste. It is a curious departure from the boutique presentation of the previous items. Colgate: what peasant stuff compared to the high-end swag up to this point!

Next, a packet of 747-profile-anointed "facial tissues"—always a nice euphemism for what are likely to become disgusting snot rags, or worse.

The bulkiest object is revealed to be an eye mask, which is, as Julien describes it when he tries it on, "very dark!" Indeed, I try it myself and encounter total blackout. The elastic band fits snuggly without being suffocating. The eye mask itself is almost totally black—but not quite. The front of the eye patches advertise on the right side UNITED (with the new Continental logo), and *747* on the left. What a curious choice: one can't help imagining a flight attendant walking down the aisle of the plane at midnight, nodding in approval as thirty slumbering passengers in the dim glow of airborne somnambulant reverie all wear the correct corporate signs, everyone unconsciously agreeing upon what must be peak modern flight. (On the other hand, the inside is plain black, and with eyeholes pricked out, could make a fabulous Halloween costume piece.)

A slim item emerges, the size of a collectible baseball cards. Oh— they *are* baseball cards, but for this very aircraft model. A cover card reads:

Celebrating the *747*

By connecting us to new parts of the world, the distinctively classic Boeing 747 captured the imaginations of its pilots, crews, and passengers. As we fondly bid farewell to the Queen of the Skies, we pay tribute to its decades of service to United'.

They even *smell* like baseball cards, when I rip open the protective wrapping. I'm excited. Alas, the cards are unremarkable: blasé photographs of different vintage 747s with accompanying notes about varying livery across the decades. The introductory card tells me that there are fifteen different cards to collect: a modest, adult-scaled enterprise.

Moving on, I pull out another card: a promotional spot that says "eco-skies"—promotional material for a "Clean the World" campaign, which sets out to "recycle portions of our amenity kits and repurpose these items to build new hygiene kits." There's even a hashtag that one can follow: #SoapSavesLives. Here the impoverished world slams into the upper elite: unused squirts of hand cream and toothpaste might be graciously passed along to the destitute hoards. The insignia on the card shows a dancing figure encircled in a green helix of arrows and soap suds. It's the now universal recycling sign given a bizarre, bubbly twist.

Two more items: the first a tiny packet of antiseptic hand sanitizer gel. So minimized as if to underplay the very reality that the stuff belies: airplanes are filthy canisters of germs and sickness. Finally, and I will admit that I've been delaying taking these out: the socks. I take them out with a thumb and forefinger, and feel the grippy tread on the soles of the socks. I open them up, though, and am delighted to see yet one more time *747*—and the profile of the plane with contrails unspooling behind! Again I envision the strange shuffle of so many business class passengers passing each other in the aisles, their socks proudly flashing the model of the plane on which they soar, and in which they snore. The Polaris Business Class amenity kit has outdone itself. I cannot imagine that the British Airways Kit contains more, or more spunk, than this one.

Turning back to the magazine ad, I now feel like I've glimpsed into two different worlds, equally implicated in the late Anthropocene. One quiet and calm against the near-apocalyptic glow out the window seat; the other over-the-top abundance, a simpering commercial for the excesses of the twentieth century, for two worlds but one clientele: the makers of this era that cannot figure out how to put on the breaks.

Snack Attack

So many smaller things equally make the Anthropocene tick along. Another example: snacks, which get us through the day. A snack can be as simple as an apple or banana, or as complicated as the array of salty flavors and accompanying micro-gustatory promises proffered at the ordinary vending machine. In the sky passengers munch on miniature pretzels and tiny pouches of nuts. As I write this, sitting on a United flight from Phoenix to Houston, I am handed a disgusting looking Stroopwaffle that I am expected to gobble along with my coffee. All around me, the wrappers of these things crinkle, destined for the garbage bags that will be making their way down the aisles in a few more minutes. A few hours later, these wrappers will be in a dumpster on the tarmac or in a refuse truck leaving Houston airport, and after that, to a landfill outside of town where gulls will ingest pieces of the wrappers as they attempt to remove last crumbs. We do not talk about these things enough, the paths and accretions of our waste.

All the while: Athletes chomp on energy bars; children dip carrots and celery in tubs of hummus on the edges of playgrounds; office workers pop peanut butter cups and spoon yogurt from small cups. Snacks bridge the gap between meals and help us get through long flights, excruciating meetings, endurance runs, or boring presentations.

Not long after I wrote about Blue Apron up in Michigan, I was contacted by a company called "Love With Food," which allegedly offered monthly boxed assortments of healthy snacks. I was intrigued by their mission: For each box purchased, a portion of the proceeds are donated to food banks across the United States. It sounded innocuous enough, and even somewhat social justice minded. I offered to review the product, and my Love With Food contact pressed some buttons to initiate the process whereby one of the red boxes was loaded onto an airplane, headed to my house. This would be a different kind of in-flight snack.

A blitzkrieg issued from the sample box I received in the mail a few days later: kale chips, rice crackers, fig bars, kosher cookies, gluten-free waffles, and even small green tea latte hard candies tucked in the corner (*snacks*—really?). Here was all of the globe tucked into a tidy bright red box, a primer in cosmopolitanism couched as a simple, healthy dietary decision and laced with a touch of philanthropy to assuage the pangs of snack-guilt.

But as I sifted through the box's bewildering contents, I noticed a message on the bottom of the box: "Still hungry? Shop more at LoveWithFood.com." It hit me: this was not really about snacking so much as it was about *shopping*. Scrolling through the company website revealed it to be just that, a shop entirely like any other shopping site. Columns of options, some tantalizingly sold out. "Snack Smart. Do Good."—so the company advocates all throughout. Yet one cannot help but hear a persistent murmur beneath the Platonic overtones, a quiet mantra emanating from the rows of packaged offerings: *shop, shop, shop, shop*. It was no mere snack attack, but also a consumerist sneak attack.

We are all hungry these days. But what are we hungry for, more than anything? The strangely addictive snack of online shopping—and for goods shipped via boxes we dispose of, which in turn are full of packages we also throw away. In truth, we snack on our own consumption, which ultimately feeds the gaping trash gyres of the oceans, one of the larger collective objects of the Anthropocene.

Love With Food's website is littered with the most positive language of our time: *love, simple, smart, healthy, good, discovery.* Meanwhile, factories elsewhere hasten to churn out ever more small glittery packages to fill these red boxes, and later our trash cans and landfills. Like the return of the repressed, what is feared is pushed away—*waste, want, work, greed*—only to be revealed in even stronger terms. We're snacking our way through the Anthropocene. And as such, snacks are no mere stopover between real meals. Rather, snacks have become their own beast, something way beyond what we ever imagined could fit in such small bags, so easily disposed of. There's no such thing as a free snack.

A World-Class Airport for the End of the World

Stocking up on supplies as tropical storm Gordon loomed over the Gulf—water, batteries, food staples—I was struck by a familiar sound in the sky as I loaded bags into my car: a bank of airliners forming a loose arc as they slanted down toward the airport, descending one at a time to land. While the city of New Orleans braced for the worst, life at the airport went on as usual.

Gordon ended up missing us completely, having fizzled out after making landfall well east of the city. A few weeks later, the Carolinas were slowly recovering from the deluge of Hurricane Florence. Weeks after that, another near-miss when Hurricane Michael put the city under a coastal flood advisory. New Orleans was spared from hurricanes that year, but each torrential rainstorm still risks flooding the city—no matter what time of year. And let's not even talk about the upcoming hurricane seasons, when it is predicted that the storms could well strengthen.

By the time this book is published in 2019, the city of New Orleans plans to open a brand new, "state-of-the-art" airport terminal. The more than a billion-dollar project is currently under construction across the runway from the existing hodgepodge of concourses; $20 million of those funds were provided as an airport infrastructure grant from the Federal Aviation Administration. During the 2016 election, President Trump made it known that he aimed to improve American airports, and this would seem to be evidence of follow-through on that commitment. But building a new "world-class" terminal in this sinking city is no straightforward matter. This building project ends up revealing the precarity of the world in its current state—a world in which airports, against plenty of evidence to the contrary, may be nearing extinction.

Taxiing beside the building site over 2016, 2017, and 2018, trip after trip, I saw the structure slowly rise up out of the swamp. Its undulating glass facade snapped into place one pane at a time, and then jet bridges began extruding from them. The new airport will completely replace the existing terminal and concourses, serving as a fresh, vibrant point of entry and exit for the millions of tourists and business travelers who visit the Crescent City each year. The current airport buildings are being assessed as to their future use—but they are likely to remain vacant for some time and will probably be slated for demolition one concourse at a time.

The city celebrated its 300th anniversary in 2018, and there was a palpable sense of pride and bustling creative energy around New Orleans during this time. Air travel in and out of New Orleans Louis Armstrong International Airport (MSY) continues to rise, up 20 percent between 2015 and 2017, with another record-breaking year in 2018. The new airport gleams across the runway, promising to facilitate the flows of this burgeoning population of jet travelers in the Gulf South. The future looks bright, from the air.

Less so, from the ground. At an average of four and a half feet above sea level, MSY is by some accounts the second lowest elevation of any airport in the world, just above Amsterdam's airport Schiphol, which lies at 11 feet beneath sea level. The low elevation of New Orleans, combined with easily overwhelmed pump systems and an elaborate system of intricate levees and diversion dams controlling the Mississippi River, makes the area especially vulnerable to flooding. Meanwhile, the nearby coast is eroding at a staggering rate—roughly a football field's worth every 100 minutes. In a 2018 article, the *New York Times* reported that the federal government is retiring place names by the dozens for islands and bays that have "simply ceased to exist."

Almost an island, New Orleans is particularly susceptible to coastal erosion. The grand opening of the new terminal was pushed from February 2019 to May 2019 after the gravity-based main sewer line was found to be sagging, requiring a pressurized system with lift stations to be constructed. It's hard to depend on gravity when construction is already taking place at such a low elevation. What "ground" rests beneath is hardly firm, and it will continue to shift around and change consistency each year. Local developers even refer to the soil here as "gumbo." In April 2019, the grand opening was pushed again to an ambiguous "Fall 2019"—right in the midst of hurricane season.

With tropical storms and hurricanes intensifying each year, a tone of bitter resignation sets in here during late summer, mixed with some gallows humor. A colleague at Tulane once told me that the university had already acquired land on the Northshore of Lake Pontchartrain, to rebuild its campus when—not *if*—the city is finally submerged and rendered unlivable from a big storm. I e-mailed Tulane and a communications representative confirmed that this was pure myth—but he also assured me that they do have a robust disaster recovery plan in place. The short distance from wild rumor to measured disaster preparedness reflects a common (if often repressed) attitude here: New Orleans's days may be numbered.

Why build a new, billion-dollar airport in this place? From an ecological perspective, the site is already doomed.

MSY is hardly the only American airport undergoing significant renovations right now. In Los Angeles, LAX is in the midst of a $14 billion renovation. In New York, La Guardia is getting an $8 billion upgrade and JFK a $13 billion overhaul. By comparison, MSY's $1 billion price tag is comparatively low. But similarly sized cities to New Orleans are spending comparable, and significant, sums on airport rebuilds or remodels. Kansas City (KCI), for example, has a new, $1.4 billion terminal in the works. KCI's investment might be more secure than the others; it is far away from any coast and thus not threatened by rising sea levels. Even LAX is on relatively high ground, at 128 feet elevation—fairly safe. But up the coast, SFO and OAK are situated just 10 or so feet above sea level: both have been deemed susceptible to catastrophic inundation in the near future.

When a single airport is taken out of commission, the ripple effects can be staggering. Anyone who has been in the middle of a perfectly smooth travel day when a storm across the country snarls plans has felt this: airlines scramble to accommodate rerouted passengers, and flights get delayed due to grounded planes 3,000 miles away. Extrapolate this to entire airports suddenly rendered useless due to the unstoppable flows of a rising ocean. So while it is mostly airports in coastal cities that will be affected directly by climate change in the coming decades, other airports also will be impacted.

Of course, airport planning would not get off the ground if it took such apocalyptic forecasts into account. Building and renovations lumber on, banking on short-term gains and stubborn to reckon with the realities of life on a changing planet. But New Orleans has felt the pain of disaster, and so the new airport is an expression of tenacity and defiance. In the face of our tenuous place and the probable reoccurrence of a major storm, we're still going to build a new airport.

Symbolically, such a structure will communicate the dynamism of the city. And materially, it could drive future capital investments and professional relocations that choose New Orleans over other urban centers. The new project reflects these intertwined goals. For example, a "jazz garden" stage, set amidst green space, is planned—to feature live performances by local musicians.

Will it be "world class," as the promotional material claims it will be? That depends on what such a structure would look like and how it would function for actual humans in the twenty-first century. These are strange times for commercial flight, when passengers expect seamless transit but inevitably run into the complexities of global migration patterns and extreme climate incidents. An actual world-class airport would have to find ways to mitigate the individuated stresses of travel while also communicating a more collective truth: flight is no easy enterprise on an ecologically and economically stressed planet. Such an airport, though, would be a real downer. Perhaps a world-class airport should be humble, rather than flashy.

To that end, the new terminal itself *is* rather bland—at least, aesthetically speaking. It has none of the breathtaking peaks of Denver International Airport, none of the swooping concrete wings of Saarinen's Dulles terminal or his TWA terminal at JFK. Instead of being architecturally noteworthy, it's just fine instead.

César Pelli, the Argentine-American architect whose firm spearheaded the new MSY design, was known more for his skyscrapers: tall glass cylinders and gently conical towers. The terminal for New Orleans looks something *like* a skyscraper—but tipped on its side. The concept sketches were stirring, rendered as they were from a drone-like perspective against an inky, evening sky. The real structure, now nearing completion, looks a little less captivating. It's an airport. Nothing really stands out. We are far from the mid-century airports like Saarinen's, or even their successors, like Dallas/Fort Worth, which promised cutting-edge convenience—drive right up to your departure gate—alongside the thrills of jet flight. Now, it's just a matter of minimizing the hassle while making the experience seem somewhat planned and dignified.

Pelli is described on Wikipedia as an architect who had "no personal signature style," which sounds rather crass but I think just means that he could adapt to different locations and regional demands in terms of aesthetics and style. Still, New Orleans is renowned for its architecture—shotgun homes, Creole cottages, the galleries and balconies of the French Quarter, and so on. It seems like a missed opportunity, to have made a shiny new airport that could really be anywhere, instead of a terminal that feels like New Orleans—from the outside as well as the inside.

That problem continues inside. An Emeril-branded eatery and a Sazerac bar will peddle local fare, offerings that smack of watered-down localism. But at least it's a genuine attempt to make a bland nonplace at least *somewhat* specific. MSY's communications director, Erin Burns, told me that the new airport would try to negotiate this balance by hosting a retail mix including "local brands that are representative of Louisiana and New Orleans." The airport will attempt to represent its locality within the context of generic comfort. It's a recipe to make all types of travelers happy.

It's also proof that today's "world-class" airport cannot rely on architectural spectacle or experiential novelty. Function is more important, but not as the Bauhaus would have had it, with elegant minimalism of form following suit. Instead, Functionalism has become no-frills, done on the cheap, good enough to get the job done—for the time being. It's world-class in the most blasé, accommodating sense of the term: inside, keep passengers satisfied, but moving. Outside, offer structure without fanfare, meeting a civic and economic need for a landscape on the brink.

The results are riddled with compromise. For instance, the rental car facility—completed only a few years ago at a cost of $72 million—is located next to the existing airport and will now be accessible only by remote shuttle. This adds an extra leg to the air journey, an inconvenience for anyone who needs to pick up or drop off a rental. Then, the new terminal brags over "a single, consolidated checkpoint." The idea of consolidation sounds appealing, and indeed free movement across the concourses, after security, is a smart feature. But regular travelers will also know that when an airport has a single security checkpoint, the risks of backups, delays, acoustic pandemonium, and long lines also increase.

The idea of a "world-class" airport in New Orleans comes to mean something different than expected. The new MSY is not attempting to be "America's friendliest airport," like the promotional material for Phoenix Sky Harbor's current near-billion-dollar renovation advertises. Nor does it aspire for the integrated smart-tech, posh lounges, or immersive regionalisms of the new airports of Dubai, Singapore, or Seoul. Yet neither is the airport responding directly to the threats of climate change, as European airports are being advised through climate science research. Here, the newness seems muted. It's as if the whole project recognizes that it is *temporary*, a quiet nod to the fragile world the airport services—even as it also gestures toward an imagined world of ever-increasing flights and booming economic potential.

If it gets flooded or destroyed in the coming years or decades, the new MSY will shimmer modestly in the catastrophe but impose relatively modest economic toll, and no great cultural loss. This is an airport for the end of the world.

The old airport terminal is still functioning, but it is slated for abandonment and eventual demolition. During a recent trip, I stared across the runway toward the new site, toward the future, where I am promised better, smoother, and more gainful transit. But then, I also know that next summer will bring another hurricane season. As readily as people will begin to use the new terminal to fly in and out of this unique city, the airport could also be as quickly abandoned.

In 1947, a year after the New Orleans airport first opened, it was flooded by the final landfall of the tenacious Fort Lauderdale Hurricane. It is uncomfortable but necessary to think about what the new terminal will encounter during its early years of operation, in these times of widespread denial of the human factor in accelerating planetary changes.

Airport construction under the shadow of climate change betrays the bullheadedness that typifies the Anthropocene. Another term for this era is "the capitalocene"—an age marked by money first, the ultimate lure for human repercussions.

Air travel is integrally tied to the accumulation and consolidation of capital, and in some ways airports epitomize globalism. They convey tourists, businesspeople, refugees, cargo, ideas, disease, and more anywhere across the globe in less than a day. This is why Trump was so eager to point out the miserable state of American airports, as he saw it in 2016. If our airports were better, everything else would automatically be better, too.

The era of climate change is also the age of the airport, in which international, cross-cultural efforts to bolster and maintain human air travel proceed at any cost. Airports both facilitate and symbolize the glory and the cost of global industry, and the global warming it has produced.

Those disturbing patterns become vivid around airports, especially those airports near sea level. But the effects can be seen everywhere else, too. Consider an abandoned airport in Athens, Greece, whose disaster porn went viral; or the eerie video camera footage of the 2011 tsunami inundating the Sendai airport in Japan, baggage carts, and Tugs washed asunder; or a "ghost airport" in Spain, deserted in the wake of the European economic crisis of 2011; or record high temperatures that grounded flights out of Phoenix Sky Harbor in summer 2017 (rising temperatures don't care about friendliness); or most recently, Typhoon Jebi's crippling effects on Kansai airport in Japan. Though certainly disparate, together these examples bespeak a looming reality of airports as shambles, with human progress entangled in their destruction at every turn. Is there any way to plan for this future, or is it simply a matter of biding time while inhabiting a world in dire straits? In the pithy phrasing of Eugene Thacker, "The Anthropocene: an accomplished ruin" (196).

New Orleans's new airport will most likely open with glee—and then it will quickly subside into the humdrum routines of daily transit. Meanwhile climate change will continue its course, an inbound vector as concrete as it is difficult to pin down. And the oceans will rise. The flight that's due eventually to arrive in New Orleans will be of a different sort than new routes or more Dreamliners utilizing the airfield. The bigger flight will be more than the new airport can ever handle. It is the impending exodus portended by climate change, a trajectory begun long ago, a terminal much longer in the making.

The Gig Is Up

It was late at night, after the keynote lecture at an Environmental Philosophy conference in State College, Pennsylvania. I was deep in whiskey-fueled conversation with Cary Wolfe about Wallace Stevens as the crowd fizzled out. The reception was over—all the drink tickets used up. Cary and I both suddenly realized at once that we had better get our rides back to our hotels arranged—before the Metallica concert let out. So long Jacques Derrida, hello James Hetfield.

Traffic had been a nightmare getting to the keynote, as cars poured off Interstate 99 toward the Penn State stadium. My friend Margret Grebowicz and I had heard about the concert at dinner, when we noticed that the restaurant was full of patrons wearing skintight black Metallica T-shirts and dark jeans. Our conference was at a strangely ornate hotel on the edge of town, the other direction from the stadium—but with only one highway to where these two paths diverged. As Margret and I drove through rain and darkness to the conference hotel, we lost our way. At times, it felt like we were driving through no world at all, except for the long line of taillights we saw in the far distance, marking the procession of fans bound for the stadium. As for us, mere philosophers ranging from the professorially disheveled to the Euro-chic, we gathered in our hotel meeting room. As we listened to Cary deliver a sober, serpentine discourse concerning curious intersections where deconstruction and evolutionary biology merged and comingled, I couldn't help but think about another performance taking place, not so far away, maybe even hearing the faintest reverberations of song lyrics: "*Bulletproof! Ah, kill the truth!*"

Metallica vaguely on our minds, we all knew that after the talk we needed to disperse and get on our ways before the roads were congested again. But Cary and I got chatting about the birds in Stevens in the lobby, and before we knew it we were watching vans full of black-clad, sweaty, smiling concertgoers tromping in through the revolving doors of the hotel. We looked at each other in panic: we had blown it. We then each turned to our phones and attempted to hail our rides.

There were only a few little car avatars spinning in the void of our phone screens, off in unknown simulacral cul-de-sacs at the edge of town. Eventually we each found a driver willing to fetch us, at ridiculously inflated fares. Mine cost $50 for a quick ride to where I was staying, at a shabby hotel on the other side of town. This was the gig economy, all right: there is no world, there are only hustling Uber drivers.

A couple days later, heading home from the conference, I got another dose of the strange surge mechanics behind rideshares. I deplaned at my home airport, Louis Armstrong International, appreciating the familiar mellow vibe of the terminal and looking forward to getting home to my family. I anticipated an easy Uber or Lyft pickup, and the quick ~$30 ride home. Instead, I encountered a quite different scene as I strolled through the sliding doors beyond baggage claim.

At first it was just the regular taxi line that struck me as odd: easily 200 people were lined up waiting for taxis—and the arrivals lanes were jam-packed, barely crawling toward the exit. I hoped that this was merely the analog clunkiness of old-school taxis and ill-timed family pickups. But inside the parking structure, where the rideshares are coordinated, things were even worse. A snarl of vehicles, no line or recognizable order whatsoever, and hundreds of deplaned travelers standing by their roller bags and holding up their phones in earnest— as if in deference to some gods that were reticent to show their powers. I tried in vain to summon a ride, but faced what everyone else seemed to be facing: a glut of demand and too little supply—or rather, what supply there was had become constricted by an infrastructure that was unable to handle this confluence of rideshares, standard taxis, and ordinary airport pickups and drop-offs. The center was not holding.

All at once, something totally bizarre happened. Everyone had been clustered in the parking garage, where Ubers and Lyfts were supposed to file in and pick up their fares. But this wasn't working. In a moment of spontaneous revolt, passengers started to leave the garage: people started wandering outside this designated space and into the approach ramp, crossing the roadways, meandering through the palm trees that lined the outer edges of the parking structure, charging across the highway, dragging their roller bags behind them. And all the while, they were holding up their phones, attempting to make contact with willing drivers, rides located *just beyond* the mayhem and madness of the airport bottleneck. It looked like the zombie apocalypse.

Around this time the airport tweeted, "We are currently experiencing traffic delays on airport roadways. Please be patient." The understatement of this was in stark contrast with the chaos on the ground—a contrast that could not have been more glaring. The airport issued no follow-ups, no clarifying instructions or advice. The delays multiplied exponentially by the minute, and travelers were going rogue. By the time I found a ride, it was with an Uber driver who was having just as much difficulty syncing up to a rider, and I—having gone rogue, too—caught him well outside of the parking structure. We then inched along in traffic for a full hour before ever making it beyond the airport perimeter.

As my home airport continues its massive construction project that will entirely replace the old facilities, Uber and Lyft rides increasingly circulate around and course through the city. Planning for our new terminal commenced in 2011, and construction is nearing completion. During this time, ridesharing has completely reconfigured how ground transportation is allotted and managed at airports—and at this airport, specifically. My experience at the rideshare lot revealed the tenuousness of this arrangement, an ad hoc, improvised solution that just barely works. Apparently once the new terminal opens, rideshares will be available right at curbside. But given the demand for such services, this seems unlikely to be a workable option—particularly if a standing taxi lane also persists outside the new terminal. The ebb and flow of gig economics is not at all a controllable dynamic.

Urban centers and even suburban and rural towns everywhere are learning to adjust to the encroaching wilderness of the gig economy; but it strikes me that airports are uniquely susceptible to the whims and vagaries of ridesharing. It may be that in these spaces, the peak of mobility can slam quickly into the harsh constraints of physical space. Everything looks ordered and idyllic on the smartphone screen, where cute automobile avatars wait to be beckoned. In the real world of ground handling, where a thousand vectors continually converge at once, or vanish—and not always in neat and tidy fashion—the illusion of control and self-direction is shattered, and what emerges is something akin to the heavy metal of contemporary existence. When demand spikes and fares hike, when free selves run rampant and collide into digital gridlock, the entire fantasy of modernity collapses in an instant. We will not be able to Uber our way out of the Anthropocene.

Life on the Other World

Julien received a microscope for his eighth birthday. During a rainstorm shortly thereafter, he dashed outside with a measuring cup and scooped a few tablespoons of water from a puddle in our small yard.

He brought the water back in and placed a few drops on a slide, and then Scotch-taped another slide to the top. (This was rough science.) He spent the next hour looking through the microscope, seeing what he could see: dirt particulates, plant material, and maybe even small living things squirming around—proof of another world right outside and under our feet, replete with its own real creatures!

A week later, I noticed that the slide was still there on his microscope. I asked him about it, and he told me that the creatures were dead. Julien asked me if we could look up what the microscopic things were, now that they were lying there dead—and I sort of fumbled, not knowing how to even start. These expired, miniscule aliens were beyond my immediate grasp, much less my paygrade as a mere English professor.

I managed to distract him with another project, but the slide remains in his room, waiting for further examination. Proof of life out there—somewhere beyond and beneath all the garish surfaces of the Anthropocene.

What motivates a search for another world? What can come from it, and where can it go wrong? Here is Friedrich Nietzsche beginning his 1873 essay "On Truth & Lie in an Extra-Moral Sense":

> In some remote corner of the universe, poured out and glittering in innumerable solar systems, there once was a star on which clever animals invented knowledge. That was the highest and most mendacious minute of "world history"—yet only a minute. After nature had drawn a few breaths the star grew cold, and the clever animals had to die.
>
> One might invent such a fable and still not have illustrated sufficiently how wretched, how shadowy and flighty, how aimless and arbitrary, the human intellect appears in nature. There have been eternities when it did not exist; and when it is done for again, nothing will have happened. For this intellect has no further mission that would lead beyond human life. It is human, rather, and only its owner and producer gives it such importance, as if the world pivoted around it. But if we could communicate with the mosquito, then we would learn that he floats through the air with the same self-importance, feeling within itself the flying center of

the world. There is nothing in nature so despicable or insignificant that it cannot immediately be blown up like a bag by a slight breath of this power of knowledge; and just as every porter wants an admirer, the proudest human being, the philosopher, thinks that he sees on the eyes of the universe telescopically focused from all sides on his actions and thoughts. (42–3)

Nietzsche is hinting at the ensnarled problems of the Anthropocene, this odd blend of myopic confidence and cosmic insignificance that defines our species. I wonder about other attempts to think cosmically and in scalar ways about the Anthropocene. I see traces of this in so many unlikely objects and weird texts—they beckon to me, keys to the Anthropocene.

For instance, take the 1989 film *Honey, I Shrunk the Kids*, directed by Joe Johnston. The setup for this movie involves an inventor, Wayne Zelinski, played by Rick Moranis, who has created a machine that can shrink things. Zelinski is trying to sell the device to NASA, to benefit space exploration—and to bring him fame and fortune (things at home are on the rocks).

During his presentation at a quasi-academic conference we hear Zelinski claim, "... and given that my machine can substantially reduce the size of bulky payloads and fuel supplies, the savings to the space program would be staggering." The audience guffaws in disbelief, and our would-be world-changer is made to pack up his box of scientific props and schlep it away in shame.

In the meantime, Zelinski's kids are playing at home and end up getting inadvertently shrunk—along with the two kids from next door. The shrinking machine works after all. The bulk of the film involves the four children reexperiencing the Zelinski's backyard as a different world.

This other world appears because of the profound shift in scale: a bee becomes an unexpected and erratic airplane; a lost cookie becomes manna from heaven; an ant becomes a surprisingly sure mode of transportation; a rivulet of dog pee becomes a river, and a found Lego brick becomes a safe, unexpected shelter. The kids are on another world, in their own backyard. Adapting to the Anthropocene means being ready to see the detritus of modern life anew, to reassess the space it takes up and potentially its use value.

The more recent film *Interstellar*, too, involves a radical scale shift—if across more astronomical dimensions of time and space. The drama of this film hinges on fantastic space voyages to remote, potentially habitable planets, via a wormhole.

But somewhat undercutting the space journey in *Interstellar* is the strange moment at the end, the most visually compelling part of the film, the *tesseract*, wherein Matthew McConaughey's astronaut Joseph Cooper becomes a homunculus floating behind the books on an ordinary bookshelf—out in deep space but simultaneously back on earth, too.

Forget about the dark side of the *moon*: the dark side of the bookshelf becomes a bizarre, alien landscape—page leafs flapping in the faintest zephyrs. Cooper floats there trying to figure out where he is in the order of things, only to gradually realize that he is behind books—books on a familiar bookshelf. But the bookshelf has become uncanny, off scale, and in the wrong context. A cosmic warp in the space–time continuum is the cause of this trippy scene, but still, *Interstellar* curiously relies on a topographic trick similar to *Honey, I Shrunk the Kids*. The other world ends up being the interior space of a young girl's bedroom, and the walls of books turn out to be a place to explore in miniature, and exploded in fractals. This is a terrain rife with secret codes, unfamiliar textures, and mysterious lifeforms.

Given the STEAMy vibes of *Interstellar* (STEAM is STEM with the Arts added after Engineering), it is almost certain that one of the books on those shelves is Mary Shelley's 1818 novel *Frankenstein*, a paragon of this narrative spiral maneuver. Shelley posits a "creature" *out there* only to bring the reader relentlessly back to the weird textures of reading the book in front of them and in their hands. The agitated Robert Walton writes letters to his sister Margaret Saville along his journey to discover a north passage across the pole. Victor Frankenstein shows up, and relays to Robert (and thus to Margaret, and to us readers) the story of creating his monster—but this story is continually interrupted by interior tales, snippets of poetry, the creature's own narrative, and other interspersed missives.

At one point, Victor is recounting a letter that he received in which his father explains how he is about to deliver some terrible news: at the beginning of the letter Victor's father acknowledges that he is deferring and delaying, and yet how, "even now your eye skims over the page, to seek the words which are to convey to you the horrible tidings" (95).

We end up reading about ourselves in the deep recesses of the novel. Reading *Frankenstein* becomes something like *Interstellar*, or rather something like *Honey, I shrunk the novel*. Shelley pulls the reader far into this nested narrative adventure only to expose the phenomenology of reading as an awkward, shared baseline— anticipating, as it were, Cooper's own metaphysical reencounter with the bookshelves in his daughter's room.

If the Anthropocene is frustrating as a concept, it is in part because of the relentless backward spiral it always takes at some point along the way. We start off talking about icebergs or coral reefs or species extinction, rising sea levels and atmospheric levels—and next thing you know we're examining our own most mundane habits: the cup I'm drinking from, the daily conundrums of how to dispose of trash, what can be recycled or composted, and what will remain … the plague of dryer sheets, the hang-ups in our minds. Yet some of these hang-ups don't pose themselves *as* hang-ups, but rather as fantasy and fun. But with the Anthropocene in mind, we can work with that, too.

For me one of the most enjoyable aspects of the *Star Wars* franchise is seeing how the other distant worlds reflect or reference our own planet: the forest moon of Endor, with its giant redwoods, the utopia of a green world in perfect balance, with cuddly creatures to boot; the desert planets of Tatooine and Jakku, reminding us of our own expansive, arid environs, just barely habitable, and yet sublime, too; the icy climes of Hoth, and the Starkiller base, arctic regions that would have made Robert Walton himself swoon. Or Dagobah, that bayou country where Yoda lives, a place that looks eerily like my own backyard: home to aliens of varying times and scales.

Weirdly, in the *Star Wars* films it seems as though the more familiar the planets are, the more delightfully alluring they become—and the more gripping the action that ensues there. It is no mere coincidence that the final battle in the spinoff film *Rogue One* ends on a planet that basically resembles a Caribbean paradise. To keep laser fights interesting, simply add a beach. When war becomes a destination, this might be another symptom of the Anthropocene at full tilt—or nearing its disastrous end.

It is as if we know deep down that this place "in a galaxy far, far away" is in fact right *here*: the other world is the one we're already exploring, plundering—even ruining.

Another minor detail in *Rogue One* evinces this point. The new ship introduced in *Rogue One*, the U-Wing, was in fact inspired by and loosely modeled after the Bell Huey helicopter. The Huey is an "armed escort" gunship originally introduced by the US Army during the Vietnam War, typically outfitted with rocket launchers, machine guns, and grenade launchers. Even though the *Star Wars* films are full of combat, we seem suddenly very far from the Romantic landscapes of Endor or Hoth.

Here we find a Mobius strip between the other, sci-fi world far, far away, and a terrible era on our own planet: the ramping up of the mechanization of doom, the becoming-blurry spectrum between conflict and war, active Empire and the imperial imagination. The other world is one where we've been before, a planet on which we're all troublingly entangled. What is both enamoring and disturbing about the *Star Wars* films—and I think what makes some people not even ever want to see them, in the first place—is the close proximity to our own foibles. *Star Wars* is really a protracted story about the Anthropocene, about a human penchant for destroying planets. How else are we to understand the destructive magnitude of the Death Star, or its only slightly revivified iteration as the Starkiller Base?

Fantasies of space travel and domination are all too near, these days. Musk's SpaceX continues to successfully launch more Falcon rockets, sending satellites and other test pods into orbit while managing quite impressively to land its reusable boosters.

Meanwhile Virgin Galactic continues to develop and test the SpaceShip Two, a traditionally piloted craft that promises to take the ultra-wealthy into the edges of Earth's atmosphere for a few minutes of viewing pleasure. Here is Virgin Galactic's founder Richard Branson in a 2018 *New Yorker* article, explaining in pithy form his rationale for such costly and privileged endeavors: "I believe that, once people have gone to space, they come back with renewed enthusiasm to try and tackle what is happening on this planet."

But what is happening on this planet? It's the Anthropocene, and it's something that humans will take with them wherever they go. It's in the oceans and in the atmosphere above us, and it's spewing out of our exhaust pipes and even in our backyard, too.

We've *been* coming back to this planet, for millennia—and we're not exactly "tackling" our self-made challenges with collective enthusiasm or shared vision. Mary Shelley explored this dilemma in her infamous novel of whorled creations and creators, 200 years ago: the creature, whoever that is, is left "in darkness and distance"— but intimately among us, as well. Our visions of the otherworldly twist back onto where we are—always already on the other world.

It is no wonder that Musk's SpaceX program evokes comparisons to Boeing aircraft in their marketing material. To grasp the relative size of the Falcon Heavy, we have to make recourse to our regular old airliners, those grubby, germ-filled tubes that roar overhead hour upon hour, day after day, belching emissions into the atmosphere. Air travel is itself another world that we frequent and which freaks us out—especially when we're stuck in the midst of a long delay or cascade of weather cancellations. There's nothing more distressing than feeling stranded at the airport, sleep deprived and stretched out across painful armrests.

Or even worse, on the taxiway while your plane just sits there, with no information, no idea of what will happen. An hour in this weird place can feel like an eternity, like being suspended in a black hole. Move over Matthew McConaughey.

David Bowie may have once wondered if there was life on Mars, but are we even sure there is life on the ordinary airport tarmac? I mean, isn't it somehow telling that of all the big fixes Elon Musk has tackled—electric cars, a tunnel under L.A., trips to Mars—he won't *touch* airports? These places are utterly alien to us!

And yet still we hasten on, flying more and more each year, directly accelerating the Anthropocene. Air travel churns on, and to question it is to question all of modernity.

Final Frontiers

Over the winter holiday, while recovering from a minor operation, I caught up on several space exploration films that I'd missed while Julien and Camille were younger, and life was a blur. I saw all these through the frame of the Anthropocene—how could I not? The most ambitious human fantasies of space travel are bound up with the most mundane Earthbound conundrums.

Duncan Jones's *Moon* (2009) puts the matter of energy extraction in the forefront. It is a tale of the lone worker Sam Bell (played by Sam Rockwell) on the moon, in charge of harvesting concentrated Helium3 from the moon's thin atmosphere and sending it home to Earth. A voiceover advertisement at the beginning announces that it is the "solution to humanity's future energy needs." The entire operation apparently requires only one human—and a Hal-like robot—to run things. The only problem is that the human turns out to be a clone. Exploitation hinges on one single human, whose biopower (including emotions and memories) has somehow been converted into a duplicable worker, for endless fuel production, cells of which get rocketed back to Earth. This worker breaks down after about three years on the moon, when a new clone is awakened. Multitudes of clones await awakening beneath the lunar base. The main thrust of this movie involves an existential quandary: who is the "real" Sam Bell? Was there such a thing, or is it clones all the way down? But a more ominous subtext lies away from the main action, back on an earth that has only increased its appetite for fuel, endless fuel. The real dilemma of this film resides not in the exploitation of a laborer (endlessly regenerated), but in the terrestrial world that has seemed to learn no lessons from the Anthropocene. Even as this spare habitation on the moon reveals serious psychological cracks and fissures where fuel is being produced, back on Earth the manic pursuit for growth continues.

The 2018 Star Wars spinoff film *Solo* similarly serves as a thinly veiled allegory for petromodernity. Everyone in the story is after the hyperfuel "coaxium," which is valuable primarily because it drives the warship fleets of the Empire. The Millennium Falcon is seen in svelte form in *Solo*, custom outfitted and cared for by its then (and temporary) owner Lando Calrissian. While watching *Solo*, I realized why the halls of the lunar base in *Moon* had looked so familiar: they were Millennium Falcon-like. They're always the same, these habitat corridors: octagonal or hexagonal, weirdly lit, ambient, hiding secret rooms, padded, easy to run through, asking to be crashed into—body meets starship.

Consider the planetary environments of *Solo*: a dystopian urban dump, replete with a dingy if severe airport ("only passengers with boarding passes will be allowed through …"); a sublime winter mountainscape; a ravaged coaxium refinery, a strip mine on steroids; a wasted desert on the edge of a vast sea. And every so often, a casino—as if all these terrestrial fates are a mere matter of luck and chance, timing and risk.

After watching *Solo*, Julien and I decided to build a Lego model of the Millennium Falcon—but since we did not have the actual Lego set, we downloaded the instructions and attempted to make do with strategic workarounds and improvisations. The end result looked great, even more authentic, with occasionally rusty parts where we had to use brown pieces cannibalized from Jabba's party barge, instead of the gray pieces that the instructions called for. Following the company's instructions but salvaging from our own mishmash assortment of pieces, it struck me how strange it was to be sifting among thousands of little plastic bricks and bits—tiny fragments of the oil industry, running through my fingers. Lego has become aware of this oddity, as well, and has recently begun a campaign to replace their plastic bricks with more sustainable corn-based products, instead. The first Lego pieces being produced from this new material are, in a clever marketing gimmick, the green bricks.

Jealous for some time with me, Camille demanded that we have family movie night—and so we curled up and put on *Wall-E* for the twentieth time or so. There is no better movie for representing and reflecting on the Anthropocene than this 2008 Pixar film—even if we have failed profoundly to learn its lessons. And it has become even more profound, as it has aged. The initial zooming shot through a layer of defunct satellites, the towers of trash juxtaposed with occasionally still-gleaming skyscrapers, functionless wind turbines spinning in the post-apocalyptic breezes … the Anthropocene world picture is here, our new Earthrise.

There is a gloomy realization that settles in during the opening scene, as we follow the little eponymous trash compactor through the rubble: it's the understanding that *this* is *it*. Human civilization has culminated in an endless, tattered consumerscape of "Buy N Large" signs and abandoned retail spaces. The Axiom Starliner, where the second half of the film takes place, is the apotheosis of an Airbus, a cosmic A380-MAX, a pastiche of a ship with no bounds.

It is hard to overstate the brilliance of *Wall-E*, with its shrewd take on the Anthropocene as a condition at once profoundly quaint and inescapably severe. *Wall-E* asks viewers to wonder about whose life matters—which creatures and things count as life, and whose absence is worth grieving or mourning for. And even if the film ties these matters up neatly as the Axiom returns to a newly fecund Earth, there is no such clear pathway out of our own becoming Buy N Large state.

Gravity (2013) and *The Martian* (2015) share some common themes: astronauts overcoming adversity and the sublime loneliness of outer space. They both end up back on Earth, in a sense. Yet these two films couldn't be more different, in terms of their final lesson. Whereas *Gravity* ends with Sandra Bullock's character clutching the mud, back on solid ground at last—*The Martian* ends with Matt Damon's astronaut survivor in a pedagogical role, ushering in a whole new era of space travel with a fresh Mars mission in the offing as the closing credits roll.

The Anthropocene: it's a label for a geologic era, a stratum marked by the cumulative movements and productions of humankind. It's meant to call out humans for disproportionate impact on the planet. It's the substratum of all these films, whether they know it or not. Is the Anthropocene a scientific term? As settled Truth, totally understood? Of course not. But that's not really what *scientific* means. As a working theory based on abundant data, and which reframes one's perspective, the Anthropocene is absolutely scientific. *And* science fiction: as something to be stuck on, continually run into, stumble over—something to be troubled by. Almost like gravity.

Proceed to the Route

This terminal's days are numbered, though not many who pass through my home airport even realize it. (A sentence from the Anthropocene if there ever was one.) But around the time that this book is published, Louis Armstrong International Airport will be abandoned overnight. These plans have been underway since 2011 when the new world-class airport to serve New Orleans was first announced—one of the many post-Katrina developments aimed to rejuvenate the city. Construction commenced in 2013 and a glassy new structure already gleams across the runway, nearly complete; after the last flights and after final passengers leave the old baggage claim on whatever is determined to be the final day of operations, the old airport will be shuttered.

The next morning the terminal and gates will all be new, or at least newly located on the other side of the runways from the old terminal and gates. But the airport is not planning for major growth; at most, its aesthetic appeal is being refurbished, with some calculated adjustments for incremental expansion. In any case, the thinness of the strip of reclaimed ground for the airport—surrounded by wetlands—limits the amount of runway space, more or less, to what is already there. And so, critics of the new airport see a cynical maneuver to lure more tourist dollars to the Crescent City without doing anything significant (like incorporating an affordable light-rail system to downtown or integrating the new airport with real urban development). Another line of criticism has to do with the fragile ecosystem around the airport, and its inescapable proximity to tropical storms; the new airport will be world-class, but not ready for the end of the world.

In the meantime, the old airport bustles and flows.

When I headed there in an Uber, recently, my driver's iPhone kept trying to direct us to the new terminal; still many months from opening, the approach roads were not even finished. But according to whatever geospatial information the phone was accessing, the airport had already moved. This had started happening a couple weeks earlier, my driver said, brushing it off. But there was something unnerving about the persistent command from phone ("Proceed to the route. Proceed to the route.") as we made our way toward the familiar terminal, where the usual airliners prepared for their usual takeoff, indifferent to the new infrastructure growing up out of the nearby swamp.

The plan is for what is called a "turnkey transition": one day passengers will fly in and out of the current airport and the next morning, all flights will be based out of the new terminal. This complete and total changeover will require months of rehearsal and preparation to be successful. A company called Chrysalis has been contracted to facilitate the transition, putting on training and simulations to prepare staff for opening day. The company's name suggests a romantic, aestheticized transition, as if shedding the old form and emerging as a beautiful new creature.

I find myself lingering on the elaborate nature of this process. For the training and simulations, the airline employees and ground crew will presumably practice moving around dummy aircraft parked at the new gate areas; they will move simulacral luggage to and through the baggage handling zones, even move entire aircraft away from their gates using "pushback" tugs, all, presumably, in obedience to fictional departure times. And even as this is happening, the normal operations they are mirroring will continue on the other side of the runway, a bizarre shadow world of imitation-airport activities in anticipation of the transition to come.

As far as I can tell, the transition will necessitate an almost total duplication of everything that makes an airport what it is: security checkpoints, computerized check-in and boarding systems, informational screens, baggage services, and so much more. Ponder the incredible technological redundancies involved, the phenomenal amounts of abruptly created detritus: hundreds of CPUs, keyboards, monitors, displays, check-in kiosks, information screens, toilets, sinks, seats, light fixtures, conveyor belts; picture all the jet bridges and other infrastructure critical to servicing the actual airplanes, all of it rendered obsolete in an instant. Fully functioning equipment in the current airport will suddenly cease to be used. Perfectly useful; totally outmoded. Contemplate the eerie existential implications of this soon-to-be ghost space, an abandoned airport, still able to function—as it did the day before—but without any extant purpose.

The difference, of course, is people: before the new terminal is an airport, it's nothing but a baroque premonition; after the old terminal is shuttered, it is trash.

"Obsolescing materials seem to occupy a strange middle ground," Margaret Ronda points out in her contribution to the book *Veer Ecology* (81). The still-working objects in the old New Orleans airport waver in this nondescript realm, caught between the present and the future, basically the same things that will exist in the new terminal—still functional and still functioning—and yet they teeter on the edge of oblivion, tools, utilities, and instruments destined quite soon for the scrapyard, or an unmarked and undisclosed grave at the bottom of the Gulf of Mexico.

The airport released a "land use analysis" recommending most of the existing structures be demolished. Part of the old airport will be left intact for potential aviation-related uses or possibly for commercial real estate development. But the report is mainly focused on the land and buildings. The interior objects aren't even mentioned.

The writer Joanna Walsh once tweeted a picture from the Birmingham Airport in the United Kingdom, a blurry snapshot of the RyanAir check-in desks with a "Hello" sign above; the angle of her camera lens eclipsed the "o," so the sign appeared to read "Hell."

It's a common sentiment—flying is hell—and grasping for a better version of this experience is like wishing for an even more efficient, more elaborate Hieronymus Bosch scene. But if an airport isn't an airport without *people*, I also have the creeping feeling that airports function best without any passengers or flights, with just the routines, the timetables, the fictional schedules and departures, and placeholder luggage.

Imagine how many tickets you could sell if people weren't the size they are? How long the runways could be, if the land wasn't where it is? (Alexander Payne's 2017 film *Downsizing* played with this idea, very much with the Anthropocene in mind: miniaturized people can *all* fly first class, even as they reduce their individual carbon footprints.)

"The airport is enhancing its guest experience program to help keep enthusiasm and exceptional standards for care high," as MSY's online publicity material promises. But what do these words mean? Since "enthusiasm and exceptional standards for care" are not what travelers associate with commercial flight, we get words like "enhancement," the promise of transformation and change for the better. But can a state-of-the-art airport *really* make the drudgery of commercial flight any more pleasant? When airlines haggle for $25 baggage and other add-on fees and squeeze seating by the half-inch to cut costs? When we can readily admit that an old but still perfectly functioning airport is so much junk, waiting to be relegated to the dustbin of history?

In early December 2018, Julien and I took my sister and her son to the airport after their visit in New Orleans. We had neglected to get beignets in town during their visit—always too much to do in the Big Easy—so we decided to buy a bunch at the airport, before their flight, and did so at the West Beignets cafe that sits just inside the terminal, before security. After leaving our guests dusted in powdered sugar at the security checkpoint, Julien was parched; so we went looking for a drinking fountain. I was not about to pay premium for a dubiously sourced bottled water, but as we wandered throughout the old terminal corridors, not a single drinking fountain was to be found.

Eventually, utterly thwarted, I asked an attendant at an information desk where we could find a drinking fountain. At first, he pointed vaguely around a distant corner; "there should be a drinking fountain over there, near the restrooms … ." But when I told him we'd just tried there, he looked flummoxed; after leafing through a three-ring binder listing all the airport's sundry accommodations, he gave up and threw his hands in the air. "I can't find any," he said; "But don't worry, there will be drinking fountains in the new airport!" In the end we found no public drinking fountains presecurity, and so I finally folded and bought an apple juice for Julien.

But it was an odd reassurance, by the volunteer airport ambassador: to quench today's thirst, the promise of a new terminal tomorrow. The sentiment obliterated the extant structure, cancelling out any present bungles or missteps. The failures of the moment are rendered nothing when compared to the glorious future to come.

Beyond the delicate geography and precarious climate conditions that put the new terminal at risk, there is another lesson for the Anthropocene here. The wish for a more perfect form of air travel ends up based on a reality that is imperfect if tolerable, at best; and thoroughly implicated in our own demise, at worst. We'll die of thirst while imagining future flights to paradise.

For now, the old terminal persists, and it will continue to work right up until the moment when it will suddenly cease, when the new MSY commences its operations, sparkling and shining with all its clever design and careful planning. Ample drinking fountains and power outlets for all!

It probably *will* be a nice new airport. But because we're in New Orleans, because of the city's fraught history with disasters and recovery, I still can't help but think about a mottled future to come. It might not be immediate. After the new terminal experiences its opening hiccups and snafus—it's only an airport, after all—the "state-of-the-art" terminal will gradually settle into the usual rhythms and patterns, a "world-class" airport that will eventually, imperceptibly become just another part of the world so ambivalently scorned-and-adored by our species. So much energy, so much technology, and so much vision, all harnessed to bring about a dynamic portal for human adventure. And so much unacknowledged waste and refuse created in the process—metonymies of the much vaster hellscape that portends our doom, beyond the runways and parking structures.

A strange thing about searching for the Anthropocene: it's like looking carefully for proof of a future that is yet to come. A future that we might yet grasp in the present, or still narrowly avoid (depending on your feelings about this present moment). But meanwhile, we continue to plan for a future that looks, basically, like a (barely) spruced-up version of the present. Proceed to the route—even if it's not the right one.

Life under Boeing

For a brief time in early 2019, Boeing's homepage resembled a scene from *Dr. Strangelove*: It advertised an upcoming live feed: "WATCH LIVE: KC-46 DELIVERY CELEBRATION AND FLY AWAY"—an imposing, minimally marked gray Air Force tanker soared against a mostly blue sky. While not exactly a bomber, it nevertheless conjured the ominous B-52s of Stanley Kubrick's paean to nuclear Armageddon.

At the same time, it's just another bit of online interpellation, this time for a fuel tanker being delivered, with prompts to "learn more" and "share." I did not click over to this video, but I could imagine the scene: uniformed personnel milling around the fuselage and wings, and later the airplane taxiing out past the clear view of the camera and lifting off into the sky. YouTube is littered with such plane events, and while they may delight the aviation enthusiast, the reality is that they often involve tedious minutes of tarmac navigation.

I had originally gone over to the Boeing website after having seen an ad in the middle of an article on another site. A space capsule flashes by, then some fighter jets and other things, and alongside these images a stream of words:

It's here
Now
The future of
Airplanes
Services
Defense
Space
is built here
The future is built here
The future isn't somewhere out there
It's here

It's almost a poem. Except that it's not. It's an internet-based sales pitch for Boeing products, made to the general reader-qua-consumer. It's also a strange notion of time: the future is *built*? Well, that sort of makes sense. But the future is *here*? The future is *now*? What is Boeing asserting, in these fleeting lines? To quote Raymond Williams: "To try to jump the future, to pretend that in some way you *are* the future, is strictly insane."

Elsewhere on the Boeing site, a clickbait headline reads: "Top 5 Reasons the SLS Is the Best Rocket to Send Americans to Mars—Read Why." An accompanying image depicts a rocket on takeoff, from an impossible vantage point above and just off to the side. The image is a photo-realistic computer graphic, conceivable but completely fictional. It promotes a future to come—a branded future of space exploration and planetary colonization. It also maintains an old iconography, with its large orange center fuel tank eerily reminiscent of the now retired Space Shuttle program.

The image here is not just wishfully optimistic for the short term—as if the final matter involves simply picking the right space ship, and then we *go*. And while this picture is curiously nostalgic for a milieu in the past, it also can't be understood merely as harkening back to a time when space travel seemed more routinized, more domesticated. Instead, this ensemble represents a profoundly awkward blend of space travel futurism and internet age presentism. The only real travel happening here is from web browser page to web browser page, click to click, swipe to swipe.

Around this time, Marina Koren reported for *The Atlantic* how Donald Trump's ambitions for a Mars mission during his presidency are not at all realistic, for multiple logistical and technological reasons. Koren puts it plainly after describing what a spaceship would need to actually (safely) get humans all the way to Mars, concluding "This miraculous technology does not exist." Still, President Trump seems to believe that it is entirely possible to accelerate the timeline and achieve a Mars landing with astronauts while he is in the White House. With ad campaigns such as the ones Boeing has invested in, it's easy to see how a Mars mission could be imagined to be so close to happening—and why it might seem so urgent, too, with the machines of war assembling in the sky, just one webpage over.

Meanwhile, Boeing continues to pump out of its factories a far more mundane form of space travel, in the guise of its commercial airliners. Those buses of the sky that passengers cram into and suffer for a few hours as they are shuttled to the strained airports of the country, where TSA agents will even screen without pay, when the government shuts down. This is our actual, realized form of space travel.

On a recent flight I sat in row 14 on a relatively new Boeing 737. The seatback in front of me was scuffed and ragged, a casualty of the increasingly tight space that airlines allot to each row. The armrests on the seats were wobbly, and the carpet underfoot was already worn threadbare. I couldn't help but think of the imaginary comfort and luxury assumed in Boeing's online visions of space travel—and how their language insists that this experience is *here already*, now—just waiting to be unleashed.

But looking around me, I saw the reality of what Boeing had built: stuffy tubes with grumpy passengers, everyone looking exhausted and sick of the whole charade. The turbofans whined as we taxied to the end of the runway, and everyone settled in glumly for takeoff.

As our plane took off, I happened to see an article reporting that a new SpaceX rocket prototype had blown over in the Texas desert, sustaining significant damage. It reminded me of the opening scene of *The Martian*, where something as seemingly simple as wind derails a massively complex, long-planned space mission. That film, which imagines the 560-day survival of a lone astronaut on the red planet, gives its premise away in speeding up the tedium—all that time crunched into the formal constraints of Hollywood entertainment.

Whether for SpaceX or in a blockbuster movie, it turns out the challenges before space travel end up being utterly ordinary rather than sensational: the relative position of planets, the physical needs and limitations of human bodies, the daily weather. Meanwhile, Boeing doesn't dwell on any of this, preferring instead to annihilate the distance between a space-age future to come and the ongoing modern moment of now. And in a way, this move is clever: it will keep President Trump believing that a Mars mission is imminent, just as it bizarrely reassures my fellow passengers that we are involved in something … futuristic.

The pilots of our 737 navigated through turbulence as we left the ground in Denver, arcing toward our destination of Phoenix. The airliner creaked and the wings wobbled as we pierced the clouds. My seatmate shifted in his seat, trying to find a comfortable angle of repose in the awkward confines of our row. The flight attendants perched on their fold-out chairs, looking duly uncomfortable. The captain's voice came on over the loudspeaker, announcing an inaudible message. And we were transported, hurtled through the lower atmosphere.

In Everett, Washington, at the Boeing factory, the 737s of the future approach final assembly and are prepared for delivery to commercial airlines around the globe. New military planes amass in secret locations, threatening war in order to preserve peace. And space exploration initiatives—from Boeing and SpaceX, to Blue Origin and Virgin Galactic—rehearse age-old promises and mantras. Airliners pull up to jet bridges, load and unload, and trundle off again. This is life under Boeing. The future is here: it's the Anthropocene. And it seems here to stay, at least for now.

Degraded

I don't fly that much anymore—only when absolutely necessary for work, a few times a year. We haven't flown up to Michigan in several years. I'd like to wind my own flight paths down even further, ideally even to not flying at all. I was glad to see the Green New Deal taking on air travel: it's a mode of transportation that needs serious rethinking, and perhaps even permanent grounding. This will not happen anytime soon, but we need to be able to acknowledge the possibility—to imagine what modern human mobility might be able to look like, without airplanes tearing the sky apart. As David Wallace-Wells notes in his book *The Uninhabitable Earth*, "Complicity does not make for good drama" (149). It's messy and uncomfortable to admit that this hallmark of human progress, *flight*, might be complicit in our downfall. But if we cannot face this truth, we'll never change things.

For a while, flying commercially always seemed to deliver surprises—an accumulating sense of progress. New models of planes with innovative in-flight amenities or compelling airport architecture and passenger services. Lately these improvements have been more modest, taking shape in more power outlets for our personal devices, marginally better dining options, water bottle fill stations, or local art programs in the terminals. As I was finishing this book, Qantas announced that it flew the first "waste-free" flight—meaning trash produced during the flight, but excluding fuel-based by-products, of course. Some airports may be increasingly taking advantage of solar panels on roofs, as well as more recycling and composting on site.

But as I flew throughout the late months of 2018 and early months of 2019, I was nagged by a sense that I'd slipped back in time—or, no, that I was approaching the end of air travel, in a rapidly degraded form.

Queuing for security at the Sacramento airport, at 5:00 in the morning, I was shocked to see a security line stretching way past the engorged, cordoned snake of people, all the way back over the pedestrian bridge to the parking garage. This was well after the government shutdown ended; the scanning stations were well staffed with eager TSA agents. But for whatever reason, the security checkpoint had no ability to accommodate the hundreds of passengers who had lined up that random Saturday morning in early February to fly out of Sacramento.

Against all odds, the line of passengers wound around relatively peacefully. A low-grade vibe of resignation lingered as we marched toward the eventual checkpoint. I heard one frantic flier on the phone with an airline, demanding to be rebooked on a later flight, as he was already running late. But all in all, we just trudged along, like lemmings to the edge of a speciation departure.

The middle of the line passed beneath an odd assemblage on the ceiling, a mass of shapes I recognized as an art piece called "Chromatic Oasis," by Christopher Janney. I had stood beneath this art piece some fifteen years prior, on a docent-guided art tour of public art at SMF.

Back then, the suspended sculpture was illuminated, and it emitted sounds activated by motion sensors as passengers walked beneath the piece. Bird calls, cottonwood leaves rustling in the wind, insects.

Now this art piece was inert, and all but ignored. The sensors were not working, and the translucent geometries sunk into the passive ceilingscape, practically invisible above the snaking line of travelers.

The line to the checkpoint was a joke; and everyone seemed inured to this fact. What once existed as a curious piece of art was now no more than background clutter—akin to the weary signage and set pieces of security protocol. I was reminded of the early scene in *Solo*, when young Han and Qi'ra try to leave their home planet of Corellia in haste—a dystopian airport scene that even includes threatening if totally bland overhead announcements.

I flew through LAX that morning, on my way home to New Orleans. I had a solid hour and a half between flights, and I was looking forward to exploring the recent improvements that had been touted about the airport. But first I had to charge my phone, so I could take pictures as I explored. I decided to go to my gate and sit for a bit and read while my phone charged. One of the things LAX was supposed to feature in abundance was power outlets for passengers' thirsty devices.

I tried to walk to my connecting gate, only to be stymied—no way to get to the next terminal. I retraced my steps and saw someone holding a ragged sign: "TO GATES 20–36" or something like that. The way led to a stairwell, and then out onto the tarmac. Suddenly there I was, standing in a shallow rain puddle, next to the very plane I'd flown in on. A bus jerked to a stop and a scraggly line of us passengers were herded up and in. We drove in fits and starts toward the next terminal—the whole thing taking much longer than it seemed like it should have. I was lucky to have plenty of time to kill. (As much as I loathe that phrase, airports alone can make it feel apt.)

Finally at my gate area, I wormed my way between travelers splayed out and taking up multiple seats. Finding a seat, I plugged my phone charger into the outlet nestled between my seat and the next one. But—no reassuring buzz in my palm. No power. I looked around, and realized that no one had their phones plugged into these outlets. On closer inspection, there were power lines coming up from the ground, but they weren't hooked up to the banks of seats. A line of fifty passengers or so trudged nearby, waiting for coffee from an improvised Starbucks stand.

I wandered the gate area until I found an old power outlet in an obscure column. There, I charged my phone.

The situation at LAX summed up the problems of the Anthropocene. The airport had been promising for years to roll out renovations that would make the traveler's experience so much better—they call it "modernization," and it is apparently ongoing. But here in the moment, on the ground, the scene was abysmal. Strung out passengers, not enough power outlets, buses carting us around miserably. It was a blast from the past, stuck in the present. A future never to come.

It is no coincidence that Bruno Latour, in *Down to Earth*, describes the ecological crisis with recourse to an air travel analogy:

> People find themselves in the situation of passengers on a plane that has taken off for the Global, to whom the pilot has announced that he has had to turn around then hear with terror ("Ladies and gentlemen, this is the captain speaking again.") that the emergency landing strip, the Local, is also inaccessible. It is understandable that these passengers would press against the plane's windows to try to see where they are going to be able to attempt a crash landing … (32)

Like a directionless airplane, the airport too can feel adrift, these days. They can seem by turns more frantic or lethargic than ever. The airport is a mover of masses, and depending on the weather, the mass is either a stampeding mob or a munching multitude.

In the Phoenix airport a few weeks later, I found myself staring at a bank of black screens—ancient TV monitors that probably haven't worked for decades. Still, there they are in the concourse, as if they might blink on at any moment, announcing flights that no longer even exist.

Connecting through the Atlanta airport in the early days after Delta changed its boarding procedures, I approached my departing gate to be confronted with a jumbled snarl of passengers jockeying for position in unclear lines wrapping out into the concourse, blocking other passengers in transit. Not wanting to add to the confusion, I hesitated outside the gate area and ambled away from the lines. At this point a passenger interpellated me, "Hey *you*, are you in Main 1 boarding? *That* line starts BACK THERE!" He pointed out in the concourse, toward the very mess that I was indeed avoiding. I responded that yes, I realized the line started back there. I'd wait until it came this way, so as not to further congest the concourse. The passenger scowled at me and turned back to his smartphone. I had been chastened for not adding to the pandemonium of terminal life. Everyone (maybe me included) seemed, in the words of Lauren Berlant and Kathleen Stewart, to be "weav[ing] around the space waiting to get taken up by something and dreading it too" (93). The Atlanta airport was thick with anticipation and paranoia, inertia and outburst.

Finally, passing through the Houston airport on that same trip, I was amazed to find no recycling bins anywhere. Where—or when— was I? It was as if this airport was thoroughly oblivious to its place in the Anthropocene.

As I took these trips, Airbus announced that it would end production of the super jumbo A380. Just a year prior, the last 747s were retired by American airlines—and now this. The grandest ambitions of twentieth-century commercial flight—supersonic fever dreams notwithstanding—had been put to bed. A few weeks after this announcement, the Boeing 737 MAX planes would be grounded after two fatal crashes. In other words, the "MAX" became ground zero of modern air travel. It was all degraded. And no one was connecting the dots that a larger crisis, way beyond the scope of commercial flight, was looming.

And yet, on my final trip of 2019, as I arrived back home in Louis Armstrong International—the old airport, the new terminal opening having been postponed indefinitely—I pondered just how perfectly okay our existing airport was. Everything was working just fine. Passengers deplaned and headed dutifully to the arrivals area, the baggage claim, to catch a cab or an Uber. The airline crews turned around the aircraft, and as my ride home merged onto the highway, a new bank of flights departed above. The airport in New Orleans was working fine, but it had also been degraded and deemed outmoded. And so the new airport across the runway continued its construction into a supposedly (and utterly mythic) better future—a future oblivious to the realities of our sinking coast and climate change.

Life's Too Short to Wait

One morning in 2017 I was heading toward the back of our house to play Legos with Julien. As I approached the spiral staircase leading up to the rickety "camelback" second story, I noticed a sign that had been taped to the stairs, right at my eye level:

NO PHONES ALAWD

I knew what this meant: Julien was sick of me multitasking on my phone when I should be focusing solely on our latest building project. Could I blame him? Our smartphones can be wretched distractors, pulling us away from the people we love most, always with the lure of some new meme, an urgent notification, or the promise of a just breaking viral story. I'd experienced something similar with Camille, when I'd suggest we make a fort together. Before we'd begin to disassemble the couch Camille would preemptively proclaim, "Okay—but *No Phone!*"

My kids know something right on the surface that we learn to bury deep down: how our personal communications devices are colonizing our immediate lives. When my children beg me to leave my phone downstairs or to otherwise abandon it before playtime, they are recognizing the insidious force of this thing, and making a small claim against it. But how long will they be able to sustain these minor acts of resistance? How long before they, too, cross over the threshold—after which point it is almost inconceivable to come back? It's already become complicated, as Julien has learned over the past year how to Google image search on an old iPad; and even little Camille came up to me one day with her latest Lego creation: "Look, Papa: I made my own iPhone!" It was a gray rectangle with colorful square "apps" stuck around the surface—the resemblance to an iPhone screen uncanny. I couldn't decide whether this thing was adorable or horrifying. Are my kids already a lost cause?

I want to be careful here, because it may sound like I'm putting forward a false dichotomy between immediate reality and mediated reality—when of course they are far more ambiguous and enmeshed.

Figure 5 © *Texture 2017*.

But stick with me while I play out a scenario: If my kids intuitively know that I'm *somewhere else* when I'm on my phone, where is that place, exactly?

Leafing through the *New Yorker* magazine in September 2017, I paused when I saw an ad for a magazine bundling app called "texture."

The heading reads "Truth will make America Great Again." The background is severe black, and a mosaic of iPhones and iPads forms a loose shape of the continental United States. On each screen resides a magazine cover, a provocative headline, or a powerful display image. The message is fairly straightforward: in this era of so-called "post-truth," we need to celebrate, defend, and consume the free press in its myriad outlets and forms. Doing these things will attune us to the "Truth"—*and* will help to make America great again, *really* great again. Let's just bracket the political nuances and theological niceties of this ad, for now, and stick with a surface reading of the image.

This orgy of screens is my children's worst nightmare, if they are trying to get my attention. But there's also something creepily *off* about it: the phones and tablets are not accurately scaled—some of those iPhones are impossibly small. The verisimilitude breaks down in order to make the composite picture snap into place. And speaking of verisimilitude, what has happened to the country's topography, or the lack thereof? Mountains, plains, deserts, riparian corridors, contoured coastlines … it has all quite literally been flattened to a smooth land of screens. Instead of terrestrial ground, we are confronted with a bewildering mediascape *as* a geological layer. This ad image becomes a crystallized vision of the Anthropocene.

Such a linkage is more commonly pictured in heaps of old busted phones, or through stories of the people who scavenge through these piles looking for trace precious metals. Behind every gleaming Apple store is a wasteland of shattered metal and glass rectangles. The ad for "texture" reflects the same terrestrial reality, just laid out more jubilantly and nationalistically. Yet what is this view, this view that promises objectivity, a clear sightline onto the country in such a way what we suddenly realize the value of the truth, and can see where to find it?

To view the United States at this scale implies a perspective situated roughly 3,300 miles above (or really, *beyond*) the surface of the earth. In other words, this is not the organizational vantage point of "30,000 feet"—a favorite if flawed trope in business and leadership discourse.

Rather, this is an outlook from even higher up: perhaps the view from a spaceship heading to Mars, leaving Earth behind for good … .

The texture ad becomes an example of what I've started calling the *cellular humanities*. This is a cluster of aesthetic maneuvers and philosophical contradictions that pose the "real" or the "true" within the technocultural and *material* context of ubiquitous pocket-size computers. It's what allows smartphones to interpenetrate our daily lives, and what makes them seemingly unquestionable: we are increasingly habituated to updating software, getting the newest model, downloading the latest apps, and so on. We think of these things as *personal* technologies, as devices designed to improve our lives at an individual scale. We are not urged to think of them as covering the planet, except abstractly as "wireless" communication networks, or in metaphorical phantasmagorias such as we see in this ad.

If the so-called "digital humanities" have involved various ways of analyzing and producing texts using new technologies, with exciting or debatable results in the classroom and in research, the *cellular humanities* is something shrewder and more pervasive: it's the hegemonic acceptance of the same technologies to reconfigure everyday communications and social space to the point where we can imagine an entire country as connected by these things, with no need for anything else. Talk about a monoculture!

But now let's leave the texture ad behind, because there is another technocultural context we need to bring back into view, in order to draw out some of the implications of the cellular humanities for thinking about the Anthropocene.

One tranquil afternoon, my phone buzzed. I thumbed open the screen to see a message from Delta Airlines, imploring: "Life's too short to wait." I snapped a screenshot of the missive, because it struck me as odd. Here's roughly what it looked like:

LIFE'S TOO

SHORT

TO WAIT.

Get Started.

What's going on here? Delta is urging me to buy a ticket, to go somewhere new—to explore the world as a place full of *other* worlds. And *Get Started*: as if it is that easy.

Delta's command to "get started" in fact raises a paradox, as I am also being urged to linger here in a *present* space—that is, on my phone's screen. To search for flights, maybe make a transaction or two, to swipe and scroll. I'm being coaxed to inhabit not a new terrestrial place *out there*, but instead a miniature if also vast terrain inside the phone—or up "in the cloud," as we say.

Commercial air travel is hawked with the lure of other worlds, exotic places—so-called "destinations." But increasingly, it's the promise of seamless connectivity and screen time that is paramount. If it's not on the phone, is it even worth doing? Around 90 years ago the modernist poet William Carlos Williams offered the then radical maxim "no ideas but in things." We might adapt Williams and say that today there can seem to be *no ideas but in phones*. For all the talk of space exploration these days, we know that the most fervent location of desire right now is in our pockets, if not already in our hands.

The Delta ad is interested in places out in the world to be explored, no doubt. But it is at least equally invested in further extending this extended phenotype of our species: our habitual, routinized uses of and reliance on smartphones as bodily extensions. If an airline CEO was magically offered the opportunity to convert their entire operation to a social media platform instead of a company that serviced airplanes, my hunch is that they would probably do it in a heartbeat. It's all in the numbers.

One of the persistent themes I've tracked over the past ten years or so is how personal digital technologies have become ingrained in the weave of day-to-day air travel operations. For instance, on that recent connection in LAX I noticed power stations between each seat in my gate area; the outlet housings were present, but the power hadn't been hooked up yet. Little signs hung under each outlet that said "Coming Soon!"—as if announcing tiny blockbuster films, or a new storefront on the verge of opening. This was like the weird opposite of my son's homemade sign on the stairs.

The effort put into creating anticipation for these outlets was incredible to me. But at the same time, it's obvious. Since the turn of the twenty-first century, some of the most sweeping if subtle changes to airports have involved accommodating not passengers, and not airplanes, but *smartphones*: those little USB charging ports between seats, the entertainment programs piped by onboard Wi-Fi into your phone, airline customer service funneled through social media feeds, and so on. Our phones get more and more accommodations, while the actual seats get thinner and harder.

These days our boarding passes can be stored and scanned on our phones. Accessory kiosks and vending machines have popped up at most airports, peddling headsets, chargers, and the like—usually for exorbitant prices. Old payphone areas have been retrofitted with outlets for our new devices. Sometimes the metallic sheen and emptiness of such minimalist alcoves, landlines having been yanked out, can almost rejuvenate the aura of commercial flight's golden age. *Almost.*

Airlines urge us to connect to Wi-Fi on the plane, to stream entertainment in order to remain docile for the duration of the flight.

On one of the last trips I took, the captain concluded an in-flight announcement with, "Okay, well, I'll let you get back to your devices now." We are all would-be, blandified astronauts on our brief hops across the globe, searching for something always eluding us, thumbing our screens as frantically as the turbine fans churn the air outside.

Or, to think of this another way: Sometimes I imagine the coincidence of air travel and smartphones as a postmodern, live, and ongoing performance of Mary Shelley's *Frankenstein*: millions and millions of Robert Waltons all hurtling around the world and sharing their needy stories over Twitter, Instagram, Facebook, SnapChat. The Russian Dolls of narrative and re-presentation have multiplied beyond our wildest dreams. And the creature isn't out there in an arctic icescape, but in our very palms. Except that it *is* in the melting ice sheets, too.

As Bruno Latour puts it in his book *Facing Gaia*:

> Instead of enjoying the spectacle of jet trails in the blue sky, we shudder to think that those planes are modifying the sky they are crossing, that they are dragging it in their wake the way we are dragging the atmosphere behind us every time we heat our homes, eat meat, or get ready to travel to the other side of the world. (254)

Latour is getting at how the things we associate most firmly with progress are in fact directly hindering our species' chances of sustaining itself on the planet.

All these screens, all this activity, all this connecting … . It somehow, even in minimalist representations such as the phone-delivered Delta invitation, retains the residually modern panache of jet travel, replete with its associative connections to *space* travel, the ultimate wish image of escape. Yet where air travel swerves to being on our phones, it also all amounts to so many more or less visible compacted layers, traces of life in the Anthropocene—the ground from which our species cannot ever untangle itself. And we know somewhere in the back of our reptilian brains that these devices are amassing elsewhere, unable to be made to simply disappear. We know, too, that life is too short to wait to do something about it—but we also can't seem to stop.

In late 2018 I stumbled upon a strange story in a magazine. Here are the opening paragraphs:

> Close your eyes and listen: Water tumbles over stream-smoothed stones. A breeze rustles tall meadow grasses. Waves break against a cragged shoreline. Katydids chirp in an endless round of call and response. This isn't an app designed for relaxation. This is nature. IRL.
>
> We jokingly use the language of addiction when we talk about our attachment to our devices, denying electronic dependence with euphemisms like "multitasking" when we check email or pop onto Instagram just one more time.
>
> Throughout history, great thinkers have taken to the outdoors to refresh their minds and nurture their creative spirits. When the grind of industrialization became overpowering, the Romantics touted the virtues of the natural world. Today, technology's incessant tug on our attention and its culture of instant gratification places significant burden on the prefrontal cortex—the part of the brain that handles tasks such as problem solving and critical thinking. That repeated brain drain takes its toll, leading to distraction and reduced motivation.
>
> Fortunately, an antidote exists, and it's right outside. Research shows that front lobe activity slows down when people are out in a natural environment. And with so many of our country's wildest spaces under fire, it's more important than ever to get out and

enjoy their beauty. The more we love them, the more we'll strive to protect them for future generations. ("Into the Wild")

We might as well add, "Life's too short to wait." For, in a striking coincidence, these paragraphs appeared in an article in Delta's in-flight magazine, *Sky*, in November 2018. In a bizarrely ironic turn, the airline is telling us to *ditch* our phones—and, somewhat astonishingly, the article is using recourse to literary language and literary history to forward this cause. Literature *and* neuroscience, together—it's a distilled example of what in certain academic corners gets called "STEAM": Science, Technology, Engineering, Arts, and Math.

We might be quick to call out the gross oversimplification of Romanticism in this article and the crass recourse to pseudoscience, as well as the odd vagueness of wild spaces being "under fire." That latter phrase was particularly untimely: this issue was published as vast parts of California were literally burning, in late 2018. And the "natural environment" evoked in this passage is *anything* but clear and distinct. We are, after all, well into the Anthropocene at this point, and such a pure landscape can only be encountered as fantasy at best. In another strange literary twist, the title of this article was "Into the Wild." Jon Krakauer's book of that same name was hardly about simply "enjoying natural beauty": rather, it was about trying to escape society and dying a grisly death in the process.

Still, even with all these caveats, we can't fault Delta entirely for poetically urging us to drop our phones and to go into the other world right outside, can we? Delta is even promoting a favorite humanities chestnut, "critical thinking." In some ways, this stand against digital saturation is one of the more clearly and persuasively articulated positions that I've read concerning the cellular humanities. In some ways, it reads earnestly as the kind of message that makes me want to return to my home up in Michigan and just … be there, surrounded by what appears to be wild space. To enjoy it and preserve it—because life's too short to wait.

But in reality, Delta is merely doing a bit of judo on our sensibilities, inflating the specter of Nature in order to slyly get us to spend more time right back on the Delta app, buying tickets to *elsewhere*. After all, this is the same company telling us to occupy every minute of the flight on our screens—*not* looking out of the window, at what would have blown Percy Shelley's mind: *being with and even **above** the clouds!* Delta's pitch for "into the wild" is romanticized consumerism, at best.

On closer inspection, the whole thing is a sham: while the article tells us we're *there*, in nature, *IRL*—we're actually *reading an article*, while cruising at 35,000 feet. A breeze rustles indeed. And wait: that clever re-mark—"IRL" or *in real life*—directs us somewhere else entirely, to a place quite different than the pastoral scenes described, much less the present moment of flight: to wit, the IRL directs us back to the messaging interfaces *on our phones*. As one Instagram user puts it on their profile description, "I prefer IRL to URL"—with no apparent recognition of the irony expressed therein.

Here is one of the vicious circles of the Anthropocene: Just when we think we've attained a totalizing perspective on the problem, it turns out we're in the middle of the picture.

***

Somewhere above Kansas, cruising at 35,000 feet, and this time on a United airplane, I turned the page of my *Hemispheres* magazine and saw something that took my breath away.

I saw an endarkened urban landscape, at the center of which an airport was spread out. Twin-engine airliners were arranged around rectilinear buildings, and the whole ambiance emitted a sense of supreme order. The scene was an organizational sublime.

Figure 6 © *Star Alliance 2018.*

But looking more closely, the "airport" in this image has been grafted onto a greatly enlarged microchip. That's no airport: that's the inside of a computer, or maybe even a smartphone. The more I look at this ad, the more eerie the image becomes. For instance, there are no jet bridges connecting the airplanes to the buildings. There are no airstairs or ground crew anywhere. The airport-as-computer chip, in fact, is utterly devoid of humans. At the same time the tarmac, as it were, is pretty congested: moving airliners around this space would be a logistical nightmare. (I know; I used to have that job.)

The pale darkness shrouding the scene reflects this nightmarish aspect. Come to think of it, where is the light even *coming from*, emanating as it is from beneath one of the quasi-terminals? It's like a scene pulled from a dystopian novel, or an unused frame cut from *Bladerunner*.

The image is in fact part of an advertisement for Star Alliance, one of the premier global airline partnerships of which United Airlines is one of the founding members, thus explaining its place in their in-flight magazine. The copy in the ad reads as follows:

We're investing in technology that you won't always see, but you will notice. At Star Alliance, we're working with our member airlines to make your journeys seamless—now and in the future. staralliance.com/tech

Once again, and not surprisingly, the message of this ad is relatively straightforward: the affiliated airlines are integrating digital technology to improve the experience of flight. This could mean everything from mobile apps and digital boarding passes to cockpit avionics and air traffic control communications. It is another installment in the inauspicious canon of the cellular humanities.

The microchip ground is a usefully vague semaphore. With no real or precise technological context, it just sort of signals *progress*—progress that is at once everywhere, and mostly invisible.

By sheer coincidence, around this time I discovered another use of this metaphor, in Olga Tokarczuk's recent book *Flights*. Here is Tokarczuk describing an airline map of Frankfurt airport:

Yes, yes, the spitting image of a computer chip, a razor-thin plate. Here there can be no doubts—they tell us what we are, dear travelers. We are the individual nerve impulses of the world, fractions of an instant, barely that part of it that permits the change from plus to minus, or maybe the other way around, and keeps everything in constant flux. (179)

By extending and somewhat mixing this metaphor, Tokarczuk is able to render human travelers as simultaneously biological and technological, "nerve impulses" and part of a coded state of "constant flux."

Back in the Star Alliance ad, the minute scale of the microchip landscape is *crucial*. What scale are we on, here? The main experience being sold is that of *flight*: human bodies in airliners moving around the globe. But the scale of the digital landscape complicates this primary modality. How big would the people be, in this imaginary landscape? As it turns out, each person would be a little smaller than a single human cell. The microchip suggests a level of vision that defies the unaided human eye. It is *cellular*, in a quite different sense of that word.

At the bottom right of the picture is a slogan: #detailsmatter. The hashtag here functions as a phatic mark, announcing digital literacy and social media savvy. And yet, this hashtag is completely absurd in its nonspecificity. Search for this actual hashtag, #detailsmatter, and *nothing* air travel related will appear on your phone. Nothing. It's an utter *failure* of a hashtag, even as it functions on the ad to appear effective, even *hip*. The hashtag is a remark of the microchip on another level, promising us that we are thoroughly in the realm of the cellular, the digital—as if somewhere well beyond or beneath the scope of the Anthropocene, where consumer patterns actually matter. Here, in the land of cutting-edge digital innovation, things like climate, other species' lives, and other terrestrial realities are of no concern.

For isn't this the wish image of the ad? That somewhere out there in the (near) future, there exists an airport that will facilitate journeys that are, as the ad promises, "seamless?" But a world without seams is no world at all.

Star Alliance clearly wants commercial flight to persist basically as such, for the indeterminate (permanent) future. The recourse to microchip scale is an assurance of technological progress, but it is also asserting a weirdly static state: *now and in the future.* Such a claim is oblivious to the dynamic lifeworld that subtends all species, even through the long processes of evolution and adaptation, fecundity and extinction. Or perhaps the ad isn't oblivious, exactly; maybe this realization is nestled well within in the unconscious of the Star Alliance ad. After all, consider the name of this organization: *Star*

Alliance. What even is *that*? It sounds rather like an evil Star Wars conglomeration: Galactic Empire, First Order, Star Alliance.

The promise of another world, stable and unchanging—able to be seen in snapshot from above, or out in an unsullied wilderness—this other world haunts the Anthropocene. It's assured to be out there, with a surface ready to be landed on, enjoyed, explored. Where human relations can be renewed, made great again, once and for all. It might be accessible by a spaceship or by an airplane—but most likely, these days, just by a smartphone. No ideas but in phones. And especially phones on planes.

Adapting in the Anthropocene lately can feel like a harried reshuffling between these two dominant modes of mediation, increasingly comingling: bodies frantically in flight, faces and fingers to phone screens. Meanwhile, the world around us ruptures, surges, and splinters. To survive a bit longer, we need to change course.

Bruno Latour explains it this way in his most recent book, *Down to Earth*: "The period opening up before us is indeed a new epoch of 'great discoveries,' but these resemble neither the wholesale conquest of a New World emptied of its inhabitants, as before, nor the headlong flight into a form of hyper-neo-modernity; instead, they require digging deep down into the Earth with its thousand folds" (81). By "digging," Latour clearly does not mean frenzied resource extraction, and maybe he doesn't even mean going "deep" at all. This is instead a *surface* commitment to the materials at hand, our actual planet in its intricacies, fragilities, and webs of coshaping entities.

How to adapt *to* the Anthropocene, even to change course? This will involve breaking from the anxious impulses to bracket ourselves—from the planet, from each other, from other creatures and things. Or, put a rather different way, it might mean breaking the impulse to be always *connected*—as if connection is ever a simple act.

In the imaginary airport of Star Alliance, we see the apotheosis of both of these desires: to bracket human life off from any other lifeworld and to prioritize *connection* above all else. The Anthropocene offers a critical corrective to this wish image, reminding us of the absurdity of *both* of these impulses to become cellular.

As Mary Louise Pratt writes in the coda of *Arts of Living on a Damaged Planet*, "What is at stake … is not what the Anthropocene *is* but how it will be *lived*" (G170). The utility of the Anthropocene as a concept is that it shatters the normative frames within which human life is so often understood. Yet it is a shattering that also opens up to engagement, even adaptation.

Adapting with the Anthropocene, perhaps for more species to survive it and to enter a new era, will require a radical attentiveness to intimacies *and* distances, an attentiveness that pushes our imagination farther than we are perhaps comfortable with—which, paradoxically, means accepting something closer and more nearby than a search for life on another world, out there. It's been here all along.

Life *is* short, as Delta says. But the future is long, and there is no escaping it.

Acknowledgments

This book was many years in the making, and it changed shapes significantly a few times. Thanks to my editor Haaris Naqvi for sticking with it (and with me) as the book developed. And thanks to Amy Martin and the rest of the Bloomsbury team for all the consistently sound support at every hinge point.

Thanks to Ian Bogost for editing some of the cornerstone pieces of this book and for helping me become a better writer. Thanks to Mark Yakich, always a reliable sounding board and collaborator, tracking the Anthropocene with me at the ground level (and sometimes beneath sea level) in New Orleans. Thanks to Danielle Kasprzak for thinking through an earlier idea of this book with me. Thanks to Aaron Bady, Rob Horning, Lily James, and Michael Marder for sharp edits on essay versions of parts of the book.

Great thanks to Robert Bennett, Jeffrey Jerome Cohen, Fran Dolan, Hillary Eklund, John Garrison, Linda Karell, Greg Keeler, Susan Kollin, Margret Grebowicz, Tim Morton, Pete Olson, Scott Shershow, Stewart Sinclair, and Kara Thompson—for friendship, critical conversations, and ongoing support along the way.

Thanks to my terrific research assistants Casey Dawson, Anahi Molina, and Rayana Windom, for helping me at key moments to understand what I was writing and how to make it better. For creating the index, thank you again Anahi Molina.

My students at Loyola helped me work through many ideas in this book, providing perceptive insights as I thought about and wrote into the Anthropocene. Thanks especially to my students in Environmental Theory (Fall 2017), Interpreting Airports (Fall 2017 and Spring 2018), Writing about Texts (Fall 2019), and Genre and the Hybrid (Spring 2020), with whom I discussed some of the texts that I linger on in this book.

Finally, endless thanks to my family: Lara, Julien, Camille, and Vera. I couldn't do any of this without you. And thanks once more to my parents Susann and Jim Schaberg, who welcome us back to Michigan each summer to find solid ground again and again, even as the world teeters.

Reprint Acknowledgments

The following pieces were adapted for parts of this book:

"Terminal Obsolescence and Looking for Water in the Anthropocene," *Popula*, January 16, 2019.

"A World Class Airport for the End of the World," *The Atlantic*, October 18, 2018.

"Wheels in the Sky," *Real Life*, March 12, 2018.

"The Jet Engine: A Futuristic Technology Stuck in the Past," *The Atlantic*, February 11, 2018.

"All That's Solid Melts into Airports," *3:AM Magazine*, January 2, 2018.

"Lone Wolf Theory," *The Philosophical Salon*, October 9, 2017.

"The Secret Life of Airports," *3:AM Magazine*, September 21, 2017.

"What Is a Snack?" *The Atlantic*, April 30, 2016.

"Blue Apron and the Thing about Dinner," *The Atlantic*, January 16, 2016.

Bibliography

Abbey, Edward. *The Monkey Wrench Gang*. Harper Perennial, 2006.

Bennett, Jane. *Vibrant Matter: A Political Ecology of Things*. Duke University Press, 2010.

Berlant, Lauren, and Kathleen Stewart. *The Hundreds*. Duke University Press, 2019.

Carver, Raymond. "Nobody Said Anything." *Where I'm Calling from*. Vintage, 1989.

Clark, Timothy. *Ecocriticism on the Edge: The Anthropocene as a Threshold Concept*. Bloomsbury, 2016.

Cohen, Jeffrey Jerome. *Prismatic Ecology: Ecotheory beyond Green*. University of Minnesota Press, 2014.

Cohen, Jeffrey Jerome, and Lowell Duckert, eds. *Veer Ecology: A Companion for Environmental Thinking*. University of Minnesota Press, 2017.

Connolly, William E. *Facing the Planetary: Entangled Humanism and the Politics of Swarming*. Duke University Press, 2017.

Conrad, Joseph. *Heart of Darkness*. Chump Change, 2017.

Derrida, Jacques. "Signature Event Context." *Margins of Philosophy*, trans. Alan Bass. University of Chicago Press, 1982.

Dixon, Franklin W. *The Hardy Boys Casefiles: Death Game*. Armada, 1990.

Ellis, Erle C. *Anthropocene: A Very Short Introduction*. Oxford University Press, 2018.

Haraway, Donna Jeanne. *Staying with the Trouble: Making Kin in the Chthulucene*. Duke University Press, 2016.

Hemingway, Ernest. *For Whom the Bell Tolls*. Scribner, 1995.

Hemingway, Ernest. *The Complete Short Stories of Ernest Hemingway*. Scribner, 1998.

Hemingway, Ernest. "Up in Michigan." *The Short Stories*. Scribner, 2003.

Kerouac, Jack. *Big Sur*. Martino Fine Books, 2019.

Latour, Bruno. *Down to Earth: Politics in the New Climatic Regime*. Polity Press, 2018.

Latour, Bruno. *Facing Gaia: Eight Lectures on the New Climatic Regime*, trans. Catherine Porter. Polity Press, 2017.
Marx, Karl. *Capital: A Critique of Political Economy*, vol. 1, trans. Ben Fowkes. Penguin Classics, 1992.
McCarthy, Cormac. *The Road*. Vintage Books, 2006.
Morton, Timothy. *Being Ecological*. MIT Press, 2018.
Morton, Timothy. *Ecology without Nature: Rethinking Environmental Aesthetics*. Harvard University Press, 2007.
Morton, Timothy. *The Ecological Thought*. Harvard University Press, 2010.
Nietzsche, Friedrich. "On Truth and Lie in an Extra-Moral Sense." *The Portable Nietzsche*, ed. and trans. Walter Kaufmann. Penguin, 1977.
Purdy, Jedidiah. *After Nature: A Politics for the Anthropocene*. Harvard University Press, 2015.
Ronda, Margaret. "Obsolesce." *Veer Ecology: A Companion for Environmental Thinking*, ed. Jeffrey Jerome Cohen and Lowell Duckert, University of Minnesota Press, 2017.
Savoy, Lauret. *Trace: Memory, History, Race, and the American Landscape*. Counterpoint, 2015.
Scarry, Richard. *Cars and Trucks and Things That Go*, 1st ed.. Golden Books, 1998.
Schaberg, Christopher. *Airportness: The Nature of Flight*. Bloomsbury, 2017.
Schaberg, Christopher. *The End of Airports*. Bloomsbury, 2015.
Schaberg, Christopher. *The Textual Life of Airports: Reading the Culture of Flight*. Bloomsbury, 2013.
Schaberg, Christopher. *The Work of Literature in an Age of Post-Truth*. Bloomsbury, 2018.
Shelley, Mary. *Frankenstein*. Broadview Press, 2012.
Snyder, Gary. *Myths and Texts*. New Directions, 1978.
Sontag, Susan. *Against Interpretation*. Dell, 1969.
Szymborska, Wislawa. *Map: Collected and Last Poems*. Mariner Books, 2016.
Thoreau, Henty David. *Walden*. Beacon, 2004.
Tokarczuk, Olga. *Flights*, trans. Jennifer Croft. Riverhead Books, 2018.
Tsing, Anna L. *The Mushroom at the End of the World: On the Possibility of Life in Capitalist Ruins*. Princeton University Press, 2017.
Tsing, Anna L., et al. *Arts of Living on a Damaged Planet: Ghosts and Monsters of the Anthropocene*. University of Minnesota Press, 2017.
Wallace, David Foster. *Infinite Jest*. Little, Brown, 1996.
Wallace-Wells, David. *The Uninhabitable Earth: Life after Warming*. Tim Duggan Books, 2019.
Williams, William Carlos. *Paterson*. New Directions, 1949.
Williams, Raymond. "Culture Is Ordinary." *Resources of Hope*. Verso, 1989.

Films

Columbus, Chris, director. *Home Alone*. Twentieth Century Fox, 1990.
Columbus, Chris, director. *Home Alone 2: Lost in New York*. Twentieth Century Fox, 1992.
Cuaron, Alfonso, director. *Gravity*. Warner Bros., 2013.
Edwards, Gareth, director. *Rogue One: A Star Wars Story*. Lucasfilm, 2016.
Forster, Marc, director. *World War Z*. Paramount Pictures, 2013.
Henson, Jim, director. *Labyrinth*. 1986.
Howard, Ron, director. *Solo: A Star Wars Story*. Lucasfilm, 2018.
Johnston, Joe, director. *Honey, I Shrunk the Kids*. Walt Disney Pictures, 1989.
Jones, Duncan, director. *Moon*. Sony Pictures Classics, 209AD.
Kubrick, Stanley, director. *Dr. Strangelove or: How I Learned to Stop Worrying and Love the Bomb*. Columbia Pictures, 1964.
Lasseter, John, director. *Toy Story 2*. Pixar Animation Studios, 1999.
Lucas, George, director. *Star Wars: A New Hope*. Lucasfilm, 1977.
Miller, George, director. *Mad Max*. Warner Bros. Pictures, 1979.
Nolan, Christopher, director. *Inception*. Warner Bros. Home Video, 2010.
Nolan, Christopher, director. *Interstellar*. Paramount Pictures, 2014.
Payne, Alexander, director. *Downsizing*. Paramount Pictures, 2017.
Petrie, Donald, director. *Macgyver: Season One, Episode 6*. Paramount Studios, 1985.
Redford, Robert, director. *A River Runs through It*. Columbia Pictures, 1992.
Scott, Ridley, director. *Blade Runner*. Warner Home Video, 1982.
Scott, Ridley, director. *The Martian*. 20th Century Fox, 2015.
Stanton, Andrew, director. *Wall-E*. Pixar Animation Studios, 2008.
Stuart, Mel, director. *Willy Wonka & the Chocolate Factory*. Warner Home Video, 1986.
Zemeckis, Robert, director. *Back to the Future*. Universal Pictures, 1985.

Web Resources

(All links live as of May 1, 2019)
"A320 Family." *Airbus*, www.airbus.com/aircraft/passenger-aircraft/a320-family.html.
12, WDEF News. "Tsunami Hits Sendai Airport in Japan." *YouTube*, YouTube, March 11, 2011, www.youtube.com/watch?v=_SgCBRza8vw.
"2017 Las Vegas Shooting." *History*, A&E Television Networks, October 1, 2018, www.history.com/this-day-in-history/2017-las-vegas-shooting.

"2019 ENCORE." *Buick*, General Motors, www.buick.com/suvs/encore-small-luxury-suv.

"Airbus A330neo." *Wikipedia*, Wikimedia Foundation, en.wikipedia.org/wiki/Airbus_A330neo.

"The Airports of the Future are Here," Bloomberg, July 21, 2017, https://www.bloomberg.com/news/articles/2017-07-21/the-airports-of-the-future-are-here

"The All-New 2019 Subaru Ascent." *Subaru: Confidence in Motion*, Subaru of America, Inc., www.subaru.com/vehicles/ascent/index.html.

Allain, Rhett. "Why Phoenix's Airplanes Can't Take Off in Extreme Heat." *Wired*, Conde Nast, June 20, 2017, www.wired.com/story/phoenix-flights-canceled-heat/.

"Aviation Consulting for Airports." *Chrysalis Global Aviation*, Chrysalis Global, 2019, www.chrysalisglobal.com/industries/aviation-consulting/.

Bachman, Justin. "The Airports of the Future Are Here." *Bloomberg*, Bloomberg, July 21, 2017, www.bloomberg.com/news/articles/2017-07-21/the-airports-of-the-future-are-here.

Baskas, Harriet. "Now Showing: Movies at the Airport." *USA Today*, Gannett Satellite Information Network, March 17, 2017, www.usatoday.com/story/travel/flights/2017/03/08/airport-movie-theaters/98869346/.

Blake, Aaron. "The First Trump-Clinton Presidential Debate Transcript, Annotated." *The Washington Post*, WP Company, September 26, 2016, www.washingtonpost.com/news/the-fix/wp/2016/09/26/the-first-trump-clinton-presidential-debate-transcript-annotated/?noredirect=on&utm_term=.10d1dca7cf93.

Blakeman, Tori. "Is the Flying Car Ready for Takeoff?" *The Guardian*, Guardian News and Media, September 10, 2017, www.theguardian.com/technology/2017/sep/10/are-flying-cars-ready-for-takeoff.

Blue Apron: Fresh Ingredients, Original Recipes, Delivered to You, Blue Apron, www.blueapron.com/.

"Boeing Next-Generation 737." *Boeing*, Boeing, www.boeing.com/commercial/737ng/.

"Boeing 787 Dreamliner." *Wikipedia*, Wikimedia Foundation, en.wikipedia.org/wiki/Boeing_787_Dreamliner.

Bogost, Ian. "How Driverless Cars Will Change the Feel of Cities." *The Atlantic*, TheAtlantic.com, November 15, 2017, www.theatlantic.com/technology/archive/2017/11/life-in-a-driverless-city/545822/.

Bogost, Ian. "How the Tesla Killed Automotive Glamour." *The Atlantic*, TheAtlantic.com, September 29, 2015, www.theatlantic.com/technology/archive/2015/09/the-car-that-killed-glamour/407248/.

Bogost, Ian. "What Is Object-Oriented Ontology? A Definition for Ordinary Folk." *Ian Bogost*, bogost.com/writing/blog/what_is_ objectoriented_ontolog/.

"British Aerospace 146." *Wikipedia*, Wikimedia Foundation, en.wikipedia.org/wiki/British_Aerospace_14.

Burbidge, Rachel. "Adapting European Airports to a Changing Climate." *Science Direct*, Elsevier, June 27, 2016, www.sciencedirect.com/science/article/pii/S2352146516300369.

Burns, Erin. "City, New Orleans Aviation Board Secures $35 Million in Additional Funding for New Terminal Construction Project." *Louis Armstrong New Orleans International Airport*, Louis Armstrong New Orleans International Airport, September 20, 2018, mailchi.mp/d1e62d613316/city-new-orleans-aviation-board-secures-35-million-in-additional-fundingfor-new-terminal-construction-project-1208485.

Calder, Simon. "Christmas Flight Chaos as Engine Failures Risk Grounding Thousands of Passengers." *Independent*, Independent Digital News and Media, December 14, 2017, www.independent.co.uk/travel/news-and-advice/christmas-flight-cancellations-rolls-royce-trent-1000-engine-turbine-blade-failure-boeing-787-air-a8099201.html.

Campanella, Richard. "How Humans Sank New Orleans." *The Atlantic*, TheAtlantic.com, February 6, 2018, www.theatlantic.com/technology/archive/2018/02/how-humans-sank-new-orleans/552323/.

Carey, Susan. "Why a Single Failed Router Can Ground a Thousand Flights." *The Wall Street Journal*, Dow Jones & Company, March 17, 2017, www.wsj.com/articles/why-a-single-failed-router- can-ground-a-thousand-flights-1489743001.

"César Pelli." *Wikipedia*, Wikimedia Foundation, en.wikipedia.org/wiki/César_Pelli.

Chang, Alenda. "Surface Tensions: Environmental Narcissism in the Age of Man." *Media Fields Journal*. May 2018. http://mediafieldsjournal.org/surface-tensions/.

Chang, Kenneth. "Falcon Heavy, in a Roar of Thunder, Carries SpaceX's Ambition Into Orbit." *The New York Times*, The New York Times, February 6, 2018, .www.nytimes.com/2018/02/06/science/falcon-heavy-spacex-launch.html.

"CityAirbus Demonstrator Passes Major Propulsion Testing Milestone." *Airbus*, Airbus S.A.S., www.airbus.com/newsroom/press-releases/en/2017/10/cityairbus-demonstrator-passes-major-propulsion-testing-mileston.html.

"Existing Terminal Redevelopment." *The New MSY*, Louis Armstrong New Orleans International Airport, 2019, www.thenewmsy.com/the-plan/existing-terminal.

"Falcon Heavy." *SpaceX*, SpaceX, November 16, 2012, www.spacex.com/falcon-heavy.

"Fearless Innovation." *Innovation & Concept Vehicles*, Terrafugia, terrafugia.com/who-we-are/tf-x/.

Frosch, Dan, and Kirk Johnson. "Gunman Kills 12 in Colorado, Reviving Gun Debate." *The New York Times*, The New York Times, July 20, 2012, www.nytimes.com/2012/07/21/us/shooting-at-colorado-theater-showing-batman-movie.html.

"The Future Is Built Here." *Boeing*, Boeing, 2018, http://www.boeing.com/space/.

Gamerman, Amy. "How the Rich Fish." *The Wall Street Journal*, Dow Jones & Company, June 1, 2017, www.wsj.com/articles/how-the-rich-fish-1496329479.

Hemispheres, United Airlines, www.unitedmags.com/.

Home Edible Grand Traverse, Edible Communities, ediblegrandetraverse.ediblecommunities.com/.

"Into the Wild." Gina DeCaprio Vercesi. "Everyone Needs Some Time Off the Grid." pressfolios-production.s3.amazonaws.com/uploads/story/story_pdf/322017/3220171546616440.pdf.

Ip, Greg. "The World Is Getting Quietly, Relentlessly Better." *The Wall Street Journal*, Dow Jones & Company, January 2, 2019, www.wsj.com/articles/the-world-is-getting-quietly-relentlessly-better-11546430400.

Kasarda, John D. http://aerotropolis.com/.

Koren, Marina. "A Triumphant First Launch for Elon Musk's Giant Rocket." *The Atlantic*, TheAtlantic.com, February 8, 2018, www.theatlantic.com/science/archive/2018/02/spacex-falcon-heavy-launch-watch/552407/.

Koren, Marina. "The Symbolism of Elon Musk Sending a Car into Space." *The Atlantic*, TheAtlantic.com, February 6, 2018, www.theatlantic.com/science/archive/2018/02/the-symbolism-of-elon-musk-sending-a-car-into-space/552479/.

Koren, Marina. "Trump's Space Ambitions Are Too Big for One President." *The Atlantic*, TheAtlantic.com, January 24, 2019, www.theatlantic.com/science/archive/2019/01/trump-mars-nasa-moon/581023/.

Koren, Marina. "Where Is Elon Musk's Space Tesla Actually Going?" *The Atlantic*, TheAtlantic.com, February 8, 2018, www.theatlantic.com/science/archive/2018/02/tesla-elon-musk-mars-spacex-asteroid-belt/552719/.

Kottasova, Ivana. "Electric Planes: European Firms Target Test Flight in 2020." *CNN Business*, Cable News Network, November 28, 2017, money.cnn.com/2017/11/28/technology/electric-plane-siemens-airbus-rolls-royce/index.html.

Kunkel, Benjamin. "The Capitalocene." *London Review of Books*, LRB Limited, March 2, 2017, www.lrb.co.uk/v39/n05/benjamin-kunkel/the-capitalocene.

Larino, Jennifer. "Take a Look Inside New Orleans' New $1 Billion Airport Terminal." *Nola.com*, Advance Local Media, December 23, 2018, expo.nola.com/news/erry-2018/12/6f3fc1cb566126/take-a-look-inside-new-orleans.html.

Larino, Jennifer. "11 Things You Need to Know about New Orleans' New Airport Terminal, Opening in 2019." *Nola.com*, Advance Local Media, June

26, 2018, expo.nola.com/news/erry-2018/06/7f04bbf1a12564/new_orleans_is_getting_a_new_a.html.

Leslie, Jacques. "California Faces a Cascade of Catastrophes as Sea Level Rises." *Los Angeles Times*, Los Angeles Times, January 24, 2018, www.latimes.com/opinion/op-ed/la-oe-leslie-sea-level-rise-california-20180124-story.html.

Meyer, Robinson. "Does Harvey Represent a New Normal for Hurricanes?" *The Atlantic*, TheAtlantic.com, August 29, 2017, www.theatlantic.com/science/archive/2017/08/hurricanes-harvey-climate-change/538262/.

Michigan Emerging Disease Issues. "How to Report Sick or Dead Wildlife." May 9, 2019. https://www.michigan.gov/emergingdiseases/0,4579,7-186-135830-,00.html

Miller, S. A. "Trump Vows Overhaul of Airports, Says Infrastructure 'Obsolete.'" *The Washington Times*, The Washington Times, February 9, 2017, www.washingtontimes.com/news/2017/feb/9/donald-trump-vows-overhaul-airports/.

Moran, Lee. "Spain's Ghost Airport: The 1BILLION Transport Hub Closed after Just Three Years That's Now Falling into Rack and Ruin." *Daily Mail Online*, Associated Newspapers, July 9, 2012, www.dailymail.co.uk/news/article-2170886/Spains-ghost-airport-The-1BILLION-transport-hub-closed-just-years-thats-falling-rack-ruin.html.

"The Overnight Move." *The New MSY*, Louis Armstrong New Orleans International Airport, www.thenewmsy.com/the-plan/the-overnight-move.

"Passenger Traffic at New Orleans Airport Continues to Climb with Another Record-Breaking Year." Louis Armstrong New Orleans International Airport, Louis Armstrong New Orleans International Airport, February 23, 2018, www.flymsy.com/press-room/Passenger-Traffic-at-New-Orleans-Airport-Continues-to-Climb-with-another-Record-Breaking-Year.

Patagonia Outdoor Clothing & Gear, www.patagonia.com/home/.

Petrany, Mate. "Athens' Abandoned International Airport Is Incredibly Creepy." *Jalopnik*, Gizmodo Media Company, July 16, 2014, jalopnik.com/athens-abandoned-international-airport-is-greek-history-1605936877.

Sack, Kevin, and John Schwartz. "Left to Louisiana's Tides, a Village Fights for Time." *The New York Times*, The New York Times Company, February 24, 2018, www.nytimes.com/interactive/2018/02/24/us/jean-lafitte-floodwaters.html.

Sayre, Katherine. "Tech Company to Bring 2,000 Jobs to New Orleans." *Nola.com*, NOLA Media Group, November 13, 2017, www.nola.com/business/2017/11/software_company_new_orleans_m.html.

Schleifstein, Mark. "Here's How New Orleans' Drainage Is Supposed to Work." *Nola.com*, NOLA Media Group, August 11, 2017, www.nola.com/weather/2017/08/new_orleans_flooding_how_the_d.html.

Schleifstein, Mark. "Louisiana Land Loss, While Slowing, Still a Football Field Every 100 Minutes." Nola.com, NOLA Media Group, July 12, 2017, www.nola.com/environment/2017/07/louisiana_land_loss_slows_to_f.html.

SpaceX. "Making Life Multiplanetary." *YouTube*, YouTube, September 29, 2017, www.youtube.com/watch?v=tdUX3ypDVwI&=&feature=youtu.be.

Specter, Michael. "Branson's Luck." *The New Yorker*, May 7, 2007, www.newyorker.com/magazine/2007/05/14/bransons-luck.

Star Alliance, Star Alliance, www.staralliance.com/en/home.

"Subscription Box Snacks." *Love With Food*, LoveWithFood, lovewithfood.com/.

Tabuchi, Hiroko. "Many Major Airports Are Near Sea Level. A Disaster in Japan Shows What Can Go Wrong." *The New York Times*, The New York Times Company, September 7, 2018, www.nytimes.com/2018/09/07/climate/airport-global-warming-kansai.html.

Tovey, Alan. "Rolls-Royce Suffers Fresh Wave of Troubles with Dreamliner Engines." *The Telegraph*, Telegraph Media Group, December 7, 2017, www.telegraph.co.uk/business/2017/12/07/rolls-royce-suffers-fresh-wave-troubles-dreamliner-engines/.

"Trent 7000 for the Airbus A330neo." *Rolls Royce*, www.rolls-royce.com/products-and-services/civil-aerospace/airlines/trent-7000.aspx#/.

Tyler Bridges. "Delayed Again: Opening Date for New Terminal at New Orleans Airport Pushed Back until after Jazz Fest." *The New Orleans Advocate*, The Advocate, September 20, 2018, www.theadvocate.com/new_orleans/news/article_12951f68-bce3-11e8-b1bf-4b245ed3f94d.html.

Wakabayashi, Daisuke. "Flying Taxis May Be Years Away, But the Groundwork Is Accelerating." *The New York Times*, The New York Times, February 28, 2018, www.nytimes.com/2018/02/27/technology/flying-taxis.html.

Walsh, Joanna. "Birmingham Airport." *Twitter*, Twitter, May 22, 2018, twitter.com/badaude/status/998875864183070720.

Yamaguchi, Mari. "Typhoon Jebi Leaves Major Airport Closed and Destruction in Japan." *Chicago Tribune*, September 5, 2018, www.chicagotribune.com/news/nationworld/ct-typhoon-jebi-japan-20180905-story.html.

Index

advertisements 9, 97, 121–2, 178–9
After Nature (Purdy) 10
airportness 100
Airportness: The Nature of Flight (Schaberg) 12
airports
   capitalism 105–7, 156, 160
   existential crisis 89, 92, 100, 109, 139–40, 178
   media 11–12, 68, 90–6, 120
   obsolescence 98, 135, 153, 157–8
   patriotism 98–100, 104, 130, 136, 160
   renovation 37, 101–3, 130–3, 165
   waste 74, 110, 127, 157, 163, 166
Amazon 65, 70
anthropomorphism 2, 30
Arts of Living on a Damaged Planet (Tsing et al.) 20, 182
Atlantic, The 118–19, 160

Back to the Future (Zemeckis) 116
Big Sur (Kerouac) 27
Bladerunner (Scott) 178
Bloomberg 100–8
Blue Apron 63–5, 127
Boeing 113–15, 125, 159–62, 167
Bogost, Ian 29, 53, 118
Bosch, Hieronymus 155
Bowie, David 110, 148

camp 32–3, 83–4
Cars and Trucks and Things That Go (Scarry) 29–30, 33
Carver, Raymond 67–8
climate change 22, 58, 62, 114, 117, 135–7, 167
college 8–11, 27, 84, 107

DeLillo, Don 53–4
Democracy 99, 104
Derrida, Jaques 55–6, 138
Downsizing (Payne) 155
Dr. Strangelove or: How I Learned to Stop Worrying and Love the Bomb (Kubrick) 158

Ecocriticism on the Edge (Clark) 26
ecoterrorism 33
Eklund, Hillary 40
Ellis, Erle 22
End of Airports, The (Schaberg) 12
existential crisis 116

Facing the Planetary (Connolly) 22
Flights (Tokarczuk) 75, 90, 179
food
   Blue Apron 63–5, 127
   foraging 7, 35, 61–3
   snacks 127–9
   Sysco 44

For Whom the Bell Tolls
  (Hemingway) 85
Frankenstein (Shelley) 145, 174

globalization 18, 26, 78, 136
Google Earth 36
Gravity (Cuaron) 151–2
Grebowicz, Margret 138
Guardian, The 116
guns 17–18, 79, 147

Hemingway, Ernest 42, 50–5
Hetfield, James 138
Home Alone (Columbus) 91
Home Alone 2 (Columbus) 90–2, 94, 98–100
Honey, I Shrunk the Kids (Cundey, Johnston) 143–5

Inception (Nolan) 94
Infinite Jest (Wallace) 95
Interstellar (Nolan) 144–5
iPhone 153, 168–70

Kasarda, John 103
Krakauer, John 176

Labyrinth (Henson) 20
Latour, Bruno
  Down to Earth 6, 26, 56, 165, 181
  Facing Gaia 174
Lego 144, 150–1, 168

MacGyver (Petrie) 23–6
Mad Max (Miller) 120
Martian, The (Scott) 151–2, 161
Marx (-ist) 105–7
Mass shootings 18, 79
McCarthy, Cormac 55
Michigan
  Lake Michigan 1, 6, 13, 20, 39, 41, 45, 73, 81–3

Leelanau Peninsula 5–6, 13
Sleeping Bear Bay 1–5, 8, 13–14, 55, 76, 86–7
Monkey Wrench Gang, The (Abbey) 8
Moon (Jones) 149
Morton, Timothy
  Being Ecological 74
  Ecological Thought, The 12, 59
  Ecology without Nature 12
  Hyperobjects 58–9
Mushroom at the End of the World, The (Tsing) 88
Musk, Elon
  SpaceX 110, 114–15, 118–19, 148, 161–2
  Tesla 110, 118–20
Myths & Texts (Snyder) 32

Nature Writing 7, 37, 48–9
New Orleans, LA
  Louis Armstrong International Airport (MSY) 5, 22, 130, 139, 152, 167
  Loyola University New Orleans 12, 40, 69, 100, 184
New York Times 110, 116, 122, 131
New Yorker, The 121, 147, 169
Nietzsche, Friedrich 142–3
"Notes on Camp" (Sontag) 33

Object Lessons (series) 71
Object-Oriented Ontology 29

plastic
  microplastics 60
  recycling 18, 126, 146, 163, 166
Prismatic Ecology (Cohen) 37–8

ridesharing 139–41, 153
River Runs Through It, A (Redford) 81
Road, The (McCarthy) 16

Shelley, Mary 148
Shelley, Percy 177
social media 54, 79, 121–2, 173–4, 180
Star Wars
  Rogue One 146
  Solo 150, 164
Stevens, Wallace 137
Subaru 45, 58, 120–1
summer 5–9, 13–19, 30, 37, 42–6, 58, 60, 71–3, 86, 121, 131, 137

"Ten Indians" (Hemingway) 57
Textual Life of Airports: Reading the Culture of Flight, The (Schaberg) 12, 29
Thoreau, Henry David 52–3
Toy Story 2 (Lasseter) 93–4, 100
Trace (Savoy) 57
Trump, Donald 78–9, 98–9, 130, 136, 160–1

Un, Kim Jong 117
Uninhabitable Earth, The (Wallace-Wells) 162

Veer Ecology (Cohen, Duckert) 73
Vibrant Matter (Bennett) 2
Virgin Galactic 147, 162
Volkswagen 117–18, 120

Walden (Thoreau) 46, 52–3
Wall-E (Stanton) 151
Wall St. Journal, The 22, 81, 91
Walsh, Joanna 155
waste 7, 20, 65, 69, 73–7, 100, 127–9, 157, 163
When Species Meet (Haraway) 48, 97
Wikipedia 58, 134
Williams, Raymond 159
Williams, Terry Tempest 9
Williams, William Carlos 172
Willy Wonka & the Chocolate Factory (Stuart) 65
Wolfe, Carey 137
Work of Literature in an Age of Post-Truth, The (Schaberg) 6
World War Z (Forster) 96
writing 5–7, 9, 11–12, 22, 29, 37, 41, 48–56, 89, 109

www.ingramcontent.com/pod-product-compliance
Ingram Content Group UK Ltd.
Pitfield, Milton Keynes, MK11 3LW, UK
UKHW021901220326
469204UK00008B/115